ITALIAN
VERBS MADE EASY
WORKBOOK

Learn Italian Verbs and Conjugations The Easy Way

Lingo Mastery

ISBN: 978-1-951949-71-6

Copyright © 2023 by Lingo Mastery

CONTENTS

Preface/About the Language 1

Structure 2

Introduction 3

Pronunciation Guide 4

HOW TO GET THE AUDIO FILES 7

UNIT 1 - BASIC CONCEPTS 8

    Chapter 1 - Verbs and Their Different Forms 9

        Exercises I 11

    Chapter 2 - Auxiliary Verbs 12

        Exercises II 14

    Chapter 3 - Modal Verbs 15

        Exercises III 17

    Chapter 4 - Reflexive Verbs 18

        Exercises IV 23

    Chapter 5 - Transitive and Intransitive Verbs 25

        Exercises V 27

    Chapter 6 - Sentence Structure 28

        Exercises VI 32

UNIT 2 – PRESENT TENSES 33

    Chapter 1 - The Present Tense 34

        Exercises I 40

Chapter 2 - The Present Tense of Reflexive Verbs 42

Exercises II 44

Chapter 3 - The Present Continuous 45

Exercises III 47

Chapter 4 - Imperative Mood 49

Exercises IV 52

UNIT 3 – PAST TENSES 53

Chapter 1 - The Simple Past 54

Exercises I 59

Chapter 2 - The Imperfect Tense 61

Exercises II 64

Chapter 3 - The Past Perfect 66

Exercises III 69

Chapter 4 - The Remote Past Tense 71

Chapter 5 - The Passive Voice 74

Exercises IV 79

UNIT 4 – FUTURE TENSES 80

Chapter 1 - Future Tense I 81

Exercises I 87

Chapter 2 - Future Tense II 89

Exercises II 91

UNIT 5 – CONDITIONAL & SUBJUNCTIVE TENSES 92

Chapter 1 - Present Conditional 93

Exercises I 101

Chapter 2 - Past Conditional 103

    Exercises II 106

Chapter 3 - Present Subjunctive 107

    Exercises III 114

Chapter IV - Past Subjunctive 116

    Exercises IV 119

Chapter 5 - Imperfect Subjunctive 121

    Exercises V 124

Chapter 6 - Past Perfect Subjunctive 125

    Exercises VI 128

Chapter 7 - Conditional Clauses 129

    Exercises VII 133

Extra - Reading Comprehension **135**

Conclusion **141**

If you need motivation… **143**

Irregular Past Participle **144**

Answer Key **146**

   Unit 1 147

   Unit 2 150

   Unit 3 153

   Unit 4 156

   Unit 5 158

Extra **162**

PREFACE
ABOUT THE LANGUAGE

Italian is the product of a long linguistic evolution of the Latin language combined with the many historical and political changes the country faced throughout the centuries. This Romance language is spoken by 66 million people in the world, most of them located in Italy.

Italy is divided into twenty regions and each one has its own dialect or accent. Each dialect is a regional variant of the language which can be similar to the "official" Italian language, or use completely different words! People speak Italian, and might speak a separate dialect too.

On the other hand, there are some regions with an accent only, meaning that they do not speak an additional language, but they speak Italian with a distinctive accent. For example, in Tuscany they do not have a dialect, but a very characteristic accent.

The Italian language is recognized all over the world, thanks to its influence on art, culture, and food. We can also find many Italian words in other languages as well. Think about **pizza, pasta, opera, paparazzi...** and many others.

Besides the words, gestures are also important when speaking Italian! It might seem like a cliché, but gestures really are an international way to communicate.

With this book, we will start to discover the beauty of the Italian language, along with all its challenges that – without a doubt – you will be able to overcome with some practice and motivation!

STRUCTURE

Learning a language should always be a fun and rewarding experience. The aim of this book is to offer you a self-taught course of study that will allow you to understand the language's grammar, as well as the culture it belongs to.

The Italian language is not made up only of verbs, but they are an important part of it, allowing people to communicate properly and feel confident in their own skills.

This book will provide you with the linguistic, cultural and strategic tools to communicate in Italian. The educational progression has been carefully planned so that the student can develop a more personal experience while practicing the language, using relevant situations.

Each chapter is dedicated to a specific group of verb tenses that are commonly used during everyday life. The exercises following each section are designed to reinforce what has been learned while expanding the student's vocabulary. They are also aimed at enhancing the student's confidence and motivation during the learning process.

Ready to learn this amazing language in a fun and relaxed way?

Iniziamo! Let's start!

INTRODUCTION

Far from being an exhaustive guide to the Italian language, with this book we want to give you the tools you need to start using Italian verb tenses right away. **Take your time** in exploring the different sections – do not rush through them, but rather enjoy this journey into the Italian language.

This book is ideal for people who are just starting to learn Italian, or for those who have been studying it for a while, but would like to have a comprehensive guide about all the most used verb tenses.

We have decided to focus on the **verbs** because – as "annoying" as they might seem to learn at first – they really give you a core skill to become fluent in Italian.

Think about it: there is no sentence without a verb. Therefore, if you want to learn the language, you cannot escape them. And we want to give you the tools you need to build your knowledge and improve your skills.

The Italian conjugation might seem overwhelming, but it truly is just a matter of **practice**. Learning the verb tenses is always a challenge, but you can do it!

Try completing all the exercises, as they are structured not only to make you practice what you are learning in that given section, but also to consolidate words and rules throughout the whole book.

Also, for each verb tense, we will show you different situations where the tense might be required, in order to expand your vocabulary and let you discover some important aspects of Italian culture.

If anything, learn from the Italians: **go with the flow**, enjoy simple things, and take a break whenever you feel overwhelmed!

PRONUNCIATION GUIDE

Before starting to discover the verb tenses, you surely need a guide about another important aspect of the language: **pronunciation.** Because of course, in order to speak, you have to know how to read and pronounce the words you have previously studied.

Good news: Italian pronunciation is quite **easy,** because the words are read as they are written. That means that Italians read all the letters of a word, and this is why, once you learn the sound of the letters, you can start writing in Italian almost right away!

Let's start by exploring the Italian alphabet, which consists of 21 **lettere** – letters. To make it easier, we have decided not to use the phonetic symbols, but to show you the corresponding sound of each letter in English, along with the pronunciation of the examples provided. Learning the sound of each letter is also important because – as a foreigner – it is quite likely that you will have to spell your name at some point!

Pronti? Ready?

LETTER	NAME	PRONUNCIATION	AS IN...
A	A	ah	**Albero** (ahl-beh-roh) *tree*
B	Bi	bee	**Barca** (bahr-kah) *boat*
C	Ci	chi (when followed by vowels i-e) k (when followed by vowels a-o-u)	**Cena** (che-nah) *dinner* **Casa** (kah-sah) *home*
D	Di	dee	**Donna** (dohn-nah) *woman*
E	E	eh	**Estate** (eh-stah-teh) *summer*
F	Effe	ehf-feh	**Famiglia** (fah-mee-llah) *family*
G	Gi	jee (when followed by vowels i-e) gh (when followed by vowels a-o-u)	**Gemma** (geh-mah) *gem* **Guanto** (goo-ahn-toh) *glove*
H	Acca	[-] no sound	**Hotel** (oh-tehl)
I	I	e	**Italiano** (ee-tah-lee-ah-noh) *Italian*

L	Elle	ehl-leh	**Letto** (leh-toh) *bed*
M	Emme	ehm-meh	**Mano** (mah-noh) *hand*
N	Enne	ehn-neh	**Nuvola** (noo-voh-lah) *cloud*
O	O	oh	**Orso** (ohr-soh) *bear*
P	Pi	pea	**Parola** (pah-roh-lah) *word*
Q	Qu	coo	**Quando** (coo-ahn-doh) *when*
R	Erre	ehr-reh	**Riso** (ree-soh) *rice*
S	Esse	ehs-seh	**Salto** (sahl-toh) *jump*
T	Ti	tee	**Tavolo** (tah-voh-loh) *table*
U	U	oo	**Uva** (oo-vah) *grapes*
V	Vi Vu	vee voo	**Vacanza** (vah-kahn-dzah) *holiday*
Z	Zeta	dzeh-tah	**Zebra** (dzeh-brah) *zebra*

You may have noticed that some letters are missing in the Italian alphabet. In fact, letters J, K, W, Y, X are not part of it. You can find them in foreign words commonly used in Italian, though.

LETTER	NAME	PRONUNCIATION	AS IN...
J	i lunga	e loon-gah	*Jeans*
K	kappa	kah-pah	*Kiwi*
W	doppia vu	doh-pea-ah voo	*Wafer*
X	ics	eeks	*Xilofono*
Y	ipsilon	ee-psee-lohn	*Yogurt, Yacht*

We only have a few groups of letters that may have a more "difficult" pronunciation. However, once you learn how to read them, **il gioco è fatto!** *The work is done (you're all set!)*

GROUP OF SOUNDS	PRONUNCIATION	AS IN...
SCI	she	**Piscina** (pea-she-nah) *Pool*
SCE	scheh	**Pesce** (peh-sheh) *Fish*
GN	ñ	**Bagno** (bah-ñoh) *bathroom-bath*
GLI	lli	**Coniglio** (koh-nee-lloh) *rabbit*

Maybe one of the most difficult things when listening or writing in Italian is understanding when you have a **double consonant.** Whenever you have a double consonant, the sound of that letter becomes longer.

At the beginning of your learning experience, it is completely **normal** not to hear any difference. It will become progressively easier with practice.

Writing and pronouncing a word correctly sometimes can be very important! In fact, some words can acquire a completely different meaning when you double – or do not double – a consonant.

Examples:

- **Carro vs caro** *Chariot vs. dear*

- **Nonno vs nono** *Grandfather vs. ninth*

- **Palla vs pala** *Ball vs. shovel*

- **Sete vs sette** *Thirst vs. seven*

- **Torri vs tori** *Towers vs. bulls*

Now you can start practicing your reading and writing skills! Indeed, you will see that once you have learned the alphabet and the few exceptions mentioned above, reading in Italian is not that difficult.

Are you ready to delve into the world of Italian verb tenses?

HOW TO GET THE AUDIO FILES

Some of the exercises throughout this book come with accompanying audio files.
You can download these audio files if you head over to
www.lingomastery.com/italian-vme-audio

UNIT 1

BASIC CONCEPTS

CHAPTER 1
VERBS AND THEIR DIFFERENT FORMS

Before starting to discuss the conjugation of Italian verbs, of course, we first have to explain how to recognize a verb! In English, recognizing a verb can be quite easy. In fact, the verb is generally right after the subject pronoun – *I eat at the restaurant*. Examples of exceptions are whenever you have an adverb of frequency between subject pronoun and verb – *They often go to the swimming pool* – or a negative sentence – *We don't like fish.*

In Italian, the situation is a little bit more complicated, but not too much. As an English speaker, the first thing you would probably look for is the **subject pronoun**. Well, Italians do not usually use them.

Why? Because, as we will see in the next unit, the conjugated verb is always different for each subject pronoun. Therefore, as soon as you have a conjugated verb, you immediately know the corresponding subject pronoun, without having to specify it. We will discuss this further as soon as we tackle the verb conjugation.

For now, let's focus on the difference between the base (or **infinitive**) form of a verb – *to make,* for example – and the **conjugated** ones – *I make,* for example.

 FUN FACT: In Italian, the base form is called **infinito**. The same word also means *infinity*.

How can you recognize the infinitive form of a verb in Italian? It is very **easy**. In fact, Italian verbs are divided in three groups, and each one of them has its own infinitive form. We do not need a preposition like in English (to), but the verb ending indicates the infinitive form of a verb.

Each verb group has its own ending related to its base form:

- **-are.** Examples: **parlare** *to speak,* **mangiare** *to eat,* **cantare** *to sing,* etc.

- **-ere.** Examples: **vedere** *to see,* **avere** *to have,* **credere** *to believe,* etc.

- **-ire**. Examples**: capire** *to understand,* **sentire** *to hear,* **venire** *to come,* etc.

These are the three infinitive forms of Italian verbs. Actually, there is just one exception, but we will see it in one of the next chapters. **Niente spoiler!** *No spoilers!*

How can you recognize a conjugated verb, then? Let's talk about its "structure" first. Again, the English language has spoiled us, as the conjugated verb is almost identical to its base form.

In Italian, the conjugated verb is made of the **verb root + the ending** that corresponds to the related subject pronoun and the verb tense we intend to use.

The verb root is the part of the verb without the ending of the infinitive. For example, if we take into account **ballare** – *to dance* – the verb is made of the verb root (**ball-**) and the ending of its base form (**-are**). When you conjugate **ballare**, then, the verb will look like **ball** + the ending that corresponds to a specific subject pronoun and verb tense. As already mentioned, though, in most cases the subject pronoun will not be explicitly stated.

Examples in the present tense**: balliamo** (ball+iamo) *we dance,* **canto** (cant+o) *I sing,* **prendete** (prend-ete) *you take,* etc.

📑 EXERCISES I

1) Trova l'infinito sbagliato. *Find the wrong infinitive form.*

Example: cantare   vedere   giungere   (finira)

vincere	sapere	scriveri	giocare
partire	cucinara	vendere	preparare
illuminare	ascoltare	pulire	studiaro
vestire	cadere	cuocera	accendere
spegnero	bere	contare	uscire

2) Qual è la radice del verbo? *Write the verb root of the verbs below.*

Example: Capire ___cap-___ to understand

dormire	_____	*to sleep*	vendere	_____	*to sell*
sistemare	_____	*to fix, to tidy up*	pulire	_____	*to clean*
accendere	_____	*to switch on*	mentire	_____	*to lie*
guardare	_____	*to watch*	camminare	_____	*to walk*
controllare	_____	*to check*			

🎧 **3) Ascolta l'audio e scrivi il verbo all'infinito.** *Listen to the audio file and write the verb in the infinitive form.* (Find audio on page 7.)

_____	*to kiss*	_____	*to travel*
_____	*to live*	_____	*to learn*
_____	*to leave*	_____	*to teach*

CHAPTER 2
AUXILIARY VERBS

Let's start with a question: **What are auxiliary verbs?**

In English, the auxiliary verbs are *to be, to have,* and *to do*. But beware: When you say something like "We are American", you are not using an auxiliary verb. You are using the verb *to be* as the *main* verb of that sentence.

By definition, an auxiliary verb is used with the main verb of a sentence to express **a tense, a mood, or a voice**. In fact, the word "auxiliary" comes from the Latin *auxilium,* which means help, support. The function of the auxiliary verb, then, is to **support** the main verb.

Examples:

- *They have two siblings* –The verb *to have* is not supporting any other verb, so it is not an auxiliary verb.

- *We have said yes* – The verb *to have* is the auxiliary for the main verb of the sentence, *to say*.

- *She is waiting for you* – The verb *to be* is the auxiliary for the main verb of the sentence, *to wait*.

- *Did you meet them?* – *To do* is used as an auxiliary to form the interrogative mood.

In Italian, the concept is the same, but with a difference. The main auxiliary verbs are to be – **essere** – and to have – **avere** – only. *To do* as an auxiliary verb does not exist for a simple reason: it is not needed to form the interrogative mood.

How can you **ask a question** in Italian, then? You will be surprised to learn that it is actually very easy. You just have to add a question mark at the end of your sentence.

Examples:

- **Vai al cinema questo fine settimana.**   *You go to the cinema this weekend.*

- **Vai al cinema questo fine settimana?**   *Do you go to the cinema this weekend?*

But let's go back to the auxiliary verbs now – **i verbi ausiliari**. As already mentioned, the main ones are *to be* and *to have* in Italian. Once again, you can recognize them because, when they are used as auxiliaries, they are followed by the main verb of the sentence.

However, as we will see in the next sections, the Italian tenses requiring an auxiliary verb are slightly different from the English ones. We mainly need them when talking about something that happened in the past.

Examples:

- **Hanno preso il bus alla stazione.**   *They took the bus at the station.*

- **Siamo andati a scuola.**   *We went to school.*

- **Avevi portato il gatto con te.**   *You had taken the cat with you.*

You might have already noticed that the structure of the simple past in English does not correspond to the Italian one. But we will talk more about it in the section about past tenses.

Earlier, we said that *to be* and *to have* are the main auxiliary verbs in Italian. We do have a third one, though. It is the verb **stare**, which actually corresponds to English verb *to stay*.

How is it even possible that the verb *to stay* is an auxiliary verb? Well, we will explain it when discussing the present continuous in Italian. Just to refresh your memory, here is an example of an English sentence with a (useful) present continuous: *We are doing the laundry.*

For now, we will just anticipate that, to form the present continuous in Italian we do not use the verb *to be* as the auxiliary verb, but the verb *to stay*, as odd as it might seem. It becomes an auxiliary verb as it supports the main verb of the sentence, which would correspond to the English verb in the *–ing* form.

Examples:

- **Stanno andando a casa.**   *They are going home.*

- **Sta parlando a sua sorella.**   *He/She is talking to his/her sister.*

📰 EXERCISES II

1) Ausiliare o non ausiliare? *Is it an auxiliary verb or not? Write if the English verbs in the following sentences are auxiliary verbs (A) or not (N).*

Example: She was writing a poem (A).

I am playing basketball   _____

She is young   _____

Did you see him?   _____

You have a big house   _____

Don't smoke in here!   _____

2) Sai trovare i verbi ausiliari? *Can you find the auxiliary verbs in the text below?*

Oggi mi sento molto felice. Ho ripensato al mio ultimo compleanno e mi sono sentito molto fortunato. Sapete, ho molti amici che mi vogliono bene. Quando ho festeggiato i miei 30 anni, ho invitato tutti a casa mia per cenare insieme. Amo molto cucinare, e ho preparato la pizza per tutti! Ci siamo divertiti molto e ho ricevuto proprio i regali che volevo! Il vero regalo, però, era la presenza dei miei amici e della mia famiglia... E anche del mio cane! Sono la cosa più preziosa che ho. Adesso sto organizzando la prima vacanza che faremo tutti insieme. Non vedo l'ora!

Translation:

Today, I feel very happy. I thought about my last birthday and I felt lucky. You know, I have many friends who love me. When I celebrated my 30th birthday, I invited everyone to my place to have dinner together. I love cooking, and I made pizza for everyone! We had much fun and I received the gifts that I wanted! However, the real gift was the presence of my friends and family... and that of my dog as well! They are the most precious things I have. Now I am organizing our first holiday together. I cannot wait!

CHAPTER 3
MODAL VERBS

Let's start talking about this new topic with our usual question: **what are modal verbs?**

Modal verbs can be considered "special" auxiliary verbs, as they share the same function. They are verbs **supporting** other verbs, and we use them to express intent, necessity, ability, desire, orders, requests, possibilities...

As such, we cannot talk about modal verbs if we have only one verb: there must be **two** of them, the modal verb and the main verb of the sentence. And we have just used a modal verb in the previous sentence. Did you spot it?

Well, in English, the main modal verbs are *can, may, might, should, would, will, need to, have to and must*. If you think about it, you never use these verbs alone, but they are always accompanied by another verb expressing the "real" action of that sentence, which is always in its base form.

Examples:

- *I can swim.*

- *Tomorrow it will rain.*

- *You must not talk while eating.*

In Italian, the modal verbs – **i verbi modali** – are far less. There are only four of them: **potere** or **sapere, volere, dovere** – *can/to be able to, to want,* and *have to,* respectively.

As we will cover the conjugation of modal verbs in the next sections of the book, for now we will focus on their use in a sentence only. As in English, you will recognize them as modal verbs when you see another verb right after them. While the modal verb will be conjugated—in the present tense, simple past, future, past participle—the main verb will always be in the infinitive form, meaning that it is very easy to spot these verbs.

Remember? You can easily recognize the infinitive form of Italian verbs because they end with the suffixes **-are, -ere** or **-ire**.

Examples:

- **Posso andare in bagno?** *Can I go to the restroom?*

- **Hanno dovuto fare i loro compiti.** *They had to do their homework.*

- **Vuole diventare un medico.** *He/She wants to become a doctor.*

In the examples above, you have the modal verbs **potere, dovere** and **volere**, respectively. While the first and the third sentence are in the present tense, the second one is in the past tense, but that does not change the use of the modal verbs.

The infinitive form of the main verb - **andare, fare** and **diventare**, respectively - follows each modal verb. We also remind you that, in Italian, subject pronouns are not used unless you need to specify who the subject is or, of course, if you want to use first names.

This is why, in the third sentence, you see the option he/she in the English translation. In fact, in this instance, it could be either. It might seem confusing when you see it here, as you have a single sentence without any context. In "real life", though, the context of the conversation allows you to understand immediately whom the verb is referring to. And in case of any doubt, as mentioned above, the subject pronoun will be mentioned.

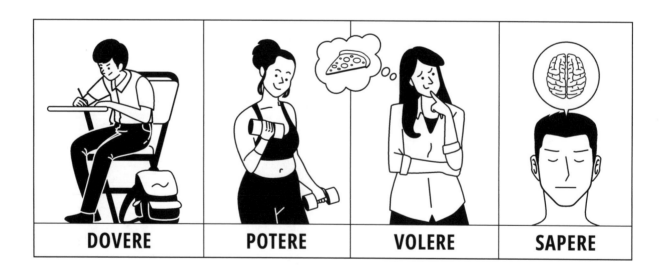

DOVERE   **POTERE**   **VOLERE**   **SAPERE**

📰 EXERCISES III

1) Qual è l'infinito del verbo modale? *Write the infinitive form of the modal verbs in the sentences below.*

Example: Possono partire domani   **potere**

Devi cantare alla festa.   _____

Vogliono andare all'università.   _____

Puoi ripetere, per favore?   _____

Vorrei un'aranciata fresca.   _____

Devo partire di corsa.   _____

Posso cucinare io, se ti fa piacere .   _____

2) Sottolinea i verbi modali. *Underline the modal verbs in the text below.*

Io e la mia ragazza vogliamo organizzare le prossime vacanze. Pensiamo di andare in America del Sud, oppure vorremmo partire per l'Australia. Abbiamo lavorato tanto quest'anno per poterci permettere il viaggio. Vorrei prenotare un volo a inizio luglio, per poi tornare tre settimane dopo, sempre se possiamo prenderci così tanti giorni di ferie. Dobbiamo chiedere ai nostri capi se sia possibile o meno. Speriamo di sì! Sarebbe il viaggio dei nostri sogni, che vogliamo fare da quando ci siamo messi insieme.

Translation:

My girlfriend and I want to organize our next holidays. We are thinking about going to South America, or we would like to go to Australia. This year, we have worked hard so that we could afford this trip. I would like to book a flight in early July to return three weeks later, assuming that we could take so many days off. We must ask our bosses if it would be possible. We hope so! It would be the holiday of our dreams, which we have wanted to do since we got together.

CHAPTER 4
REFLEXIVE VERBS

Now it's time to start talking about reflexive verbs! *What are reflexive verbs, then?*

Reflexive verbs are used to express an action done to oneself, meaning that the <u>subject</u>—the person or object performing the action—and the <u>object</u>—the person or thing that receives the action of a chosen verb—of a sentence are <u>the same</u>.

Let's look at a sample sentence like "I wash the car". The subject of that sentence is I, while the object is the car.

In the sentence *"I wash myself"*, the situation is different. The subject of the sentence is still "I", so I am the person performing the action, but I am also the object of the same action, as I am washing myself.

Reflexive verbs are definitely more common in Italian than in English. And some English verbs become reflexive in Italian. But how can you recognize them in Italian if you do not understand the meaning of a given sentence?

Easy! Let's start with their base form. Do you remember when we discussed the **infinito** of the three groups of verbs, with their endings **-are, -ere, -ire**?

As anticipated, reflexive verbs are an exception, as they do not share the same endings. Or better, they share only part of them. Recognizing them, though, will take you just a couple of seconds.

In fact, all reflexive verbs are verbs belonging to the **-are, -ere or -ire** groups, but they end with **-si** instead. They keep the first two letters of the "standard" infinitive form, but they lose the last vowel and add the suffix **-si**.

Examples:

- **Lavarsi**   *to wash oneself* = **lavare+si**

- **Prepararsi**   *to get ready* = **preparare+si**

- **Vestirsi**   *to get dressed* = **vestire+si**

Now you understand why that little **–si** is so important when it comes to the infinitive form of reflexive verbs. If you do not add it, the verb acquires a different meaning! If we look at the examples above, **prepararsi** means *"to get ready"*, but if you say **preparare,** then, you are using the verb *"to prepare"*.

As for a conjugated reflexive verb, you can easily recognize it as it is always – always! – accompanied by its corresponding reflexive pronoun – **il pronome riflessivo**. If we take the usual sample sentence – I wash myself – myself is the reflexive pronoun. There is an important difference, though. In Italian, reflexive pronouns go before the verb they refer to.

Here is a useful table with the reflexive pronouns in Italian and their corresponding ones in English. For now, we will focus on the reflexive pronouns only. We will talk more about the different subject pronouns when we start working on the verb conjugation.

SUBJECT PRONOUNS	REFLEXIVE PRONOUNS
io *I*	**mi** *myself*
tu *you*	**ti** *yourself*
lui/lei/Lei *he/she/formal*	**si** *himself/herself/itself*
noi *we*	**ci** *ourselves*
voi *you*	**vi** *yourselves*
loro *they*	**si** *themselves*

As you might have noticed, all reflexive pronouns are different apart from the ones for the subject pronouns he/she/it and they. In those instances, the reflexive pronoun is the same: **si.**

Examples:

- **Mi lavo,** *I wash myself,* where "**mi**" is the reflexive pronoun. Remember that the subject pronoun of the sentence is missing. If we want to specify it, we would have to say **"io mi lavo"**.

- **Vi siete persi,** *You got lost,* where "**vi**" is the reflexive pronoun. The complete sentence, including the subject pronoun, would be "**voi vi siete persi**".

Okay, we now know that spotting a reflexive verb is easy, whether it is in its infinitive form or conjugated. Now the question is: how can you know when an English verb is a reflexive one in Italian?

First of all, an English reflexive verb is reflexive in Italian as well. Also, many verbs including "get" are reflexive ones in Italian – as you can see from the examples above (**vestirsi, prepararsi**).

Here is a short list of some of the most common reflexive verbs in Italian, along with their English translation:

abituarsi a	*to get used to*
addormentarsi	*to fall asleep*
arrabbiarsi	*to get angry*
alzarsi	*to get up*
annoiarsi	*to get bored*
chiamarsi	*to be called*
divertirsi	*to have fun*
domandarsi	*to wonder*
farsi male	*to hurt oneself*
fermarsi	*to stop*
lamentarsi	*to complain*
lavarsi	*to wash oneself*
mettersi	*to put on*
occuparsi di	*to take care of*
perdersi	*to get lost*
pettinarsi	*to comb one's hair*
preoccuparsi	*to worry*

prepararsi	*to get ready*
ricordarsi	*to remember*
riposarsi	*to rest*
rompersi	*to break (one's leg, arm, etc.)*
sbagliarsi	*to be mistaken*
sbrigarsi	*to hurry*
svegliarsi	*to wake up*
vestirsi	*to get dressed*

Of course, the list above is not intended to be a comprehensive one. Those are the most common reflexive verbs Italians use in their everyday life.

One last thing before closing this chapter: reciprocal verbs – **i verbi reciproci.** Do not be scared! Reciprocal verbs are used when two or more people are, literally, reciprocating an action, meaning that the action is performed to one another. Reciprocal actions are, for example, *meeting each other, calling each other, talking to each other,* etc.

In Italian, reciprocal verbs behave just like reflexive ones. It means that they have an infinitive form ending with the suffix **-si**, and, when conjugated, they are preceded by the corresponding reflexive pronoun.

Examples:

- **Ci conosciamo da dieci anni.**   *We have known each other for ten years.*
- **Si sono incontrati all'università.**   *They met in college.*
- **Vi chiamate ogni giorno.**   *You call each other every day.*

Here is a short list of the most common reciprocal verbs in Italian:

abbracciarsi	*to hug each other*
aiutarsi	*to help each other*
amarsi	*to love each other*

baciarsi	*to kiss each other*
capirsi	*to understand each other*
chiamarsi	*to call each other*
conoscersi	*to know each other*
fidanzarsi	*to get engaged*
guardarsi	*to look at each other*
incontrarsi	*to meet each other*
innamorarsi	*to fall in love (you can use it even if there is no reciprocity – ha!)*
odiarsi	*to hate each other*
parlarsi	*to speak with each other*
salutarsi	*to greet each other*
sposarsi	*to get married*

📑 EXERCISES IV

1) Verbo riflessivo o reciproco? *Look at the following verbs and write if they are reflexive verbs (REF) or reciprocal ones (REC).*

Example: Prepararsi (REF)

Sposarsi   _____

Lavarsi   _____

Pettinarsi   _____

Incontrarsi   _____

Capirsi   _____

Mettersi   _____

Riposarsi   _____

Aiutarsi   _____

2) Unisci soggetto e pronome riflessivo. *Connect each subject pronoun to the corresponding reflexive pronoun.*

Io	si
Tu	ci
Lui/lei	mi
Noi	vi
Voi	si
Loro	ti

3) Ascolta l'audio. *Listen to the audio file and add the missing reflexive verbs.*
(Find audio on page 7.)

Ogni mattina mia sorella _____ alle 7, ma non _____ mai prima delle 8.

Poi _____ e va a fare colazione. Dopo _____ i denti insieme in bagno e

_____ per andare a scuola. I nostri genitori _____ alle nostre facce assonnate!

Prima che usciamo, _____ sempre.

Translation:

Every morning, my sister wakes up at 7, but she never gets up before 8. Then she washes herself and has breakfast. Then we brush our teeth together in the bathroom and get ready to leave for school. Our parents got used to our sleepy faces! Before we leave, they always hug us.

CHAPTER 5
TRANSITIVE AND INTRANSITIVE VERBS

In order to provide you with a comprehensive overview on verbs, we must discuss the difference between **transitive** and **intransitive verbs**.

First of all, every single verb is either a transitive or intransitive one. And it is important to know whether the verb we are planning to use belongs to the first or second group – more about that when we introduce the simple past!

What is the difference between transitive and intransitive verbs, then?

Do not worry: it is not rocket science. A transitive verb is a verb requiring an **object** to make sense. For example, thinking about the verb *to make,* would it make sense if we do not add a direct object?

In fact, if I just say "I make", the spontaneous question that someone would ask is "What?". The verb to make is a transitive one, as it needs a direct object. For example, I make a cake.

Other examples of transitive verbs: *to bring, to create, to phone, to send, to wash,* etc.

 Tip: If you are in doubt about a verb, try to ask yourself the question "What?" or "Who?". If you can answer that question with an object and, of course, if the sentence makes sense, well, you are dealing with a transitive verb.

Intransitive verbs are the opposite. They do **not** need an object to make sense. We can add a full stop after the verb and the sentence would be perfectly complete. Sometimes, they can be followed by other words, for example adverbs, but you will not find a direct object.

In fact, if you do find an object after an intransitive verb, it is not going to be a direct one – as in *"You send a letter"* – but an **indirect object**, meaning that the object is introduced by a preposition like "to" or "at".

We can take the verb *to arrive* as an example. If we just say *"They arrive"*, the sentence is complete and makes total sense. Furthermore, if you ask yourself the question "What?", you cannot answer. Rather, you might ask "Where?". In this instance, you can add an indirect object, as in *"They arrive at the bus stop"*. The indirect object is introduced by the preposition "at".

Other examples of intransitive verbs: *to depend, to fly, to go, to jump, to run, to smile*, etc.

 Tip: Intransitive verbs often answer the questions "How?", "Where?", "When?".

Now, let's start talking about Italian transitive and intransitive verbs – **i verbi transitivi e intransitivi**. The mechanism is exactly the same. Italian transitive verbs require a direct object, while the intransitive verbs do not have one. Most of the verbs of movement, for example, are intransitive ones.

Examples:

- **Il treno parte alle 3,** *The train leaves at 3*. The verb "**partire**" is an intransitive one, as it does not answer the questions "What?" or "Who?", but can answer the question "When?" as in this example.

- **Mio padre cucina il pollo,** *My father cooks the chicken*. The verb "**cucinare**" is a transitive one, as it answers the question "What?". In this example, the direct object is the chicken.

Here is a short list of some Italian transitive verbs:

accendere	*to switch on*	**pulire**	*to clean*
bere	*to drink*	**ricevere**	*to receive*
capire	*to understand*	**spegnere**	*to switch off*
comprare	*to buy*	**studiare**	*to study*
finire	*to finish*	**vedere**	*to see*
inviare	*to send*	**vendere**	*to sell*
mangiare	*to eat*		

And some intransitive ones:

andare	*to go*	**durare**	*to last*
arrivare	*to arrive*	**piangere**	*to cry*
camminare	*to walk*	**ridere**	*to laugh*
dormire	*to sleep*		

 **EXERCISES V**

1) Verbo transitivo o intransitivo? *Look at the following verbs and write if they are transitive (T) or intransitive (I).*

Example: Finire (T)   **to end**

Prendere ————— to take

Andare ————— to go

Cambiare ————— to change

Guardare ————— to watch

Nuotare ————— to swim

Morire ————— to die

Vincere ————— to win

Atterrare ————— to land

2) A quale domanda rispondono? *Which question(s) do the verbs of the previous exercise answer?*

Example: Prendere _What?_ to take

Andare —————   Atterrare —————

Cambiare —————

Guardare —————

Nuotare —————

Morire —————

Vincere —————

CHAPTER 6
SENTENCE STRUCTURE

Of course, in order to speak in Italian, you have to know how to structure your speech. Or better, how to structure a clause. *What is a clause, though?*

In short, a clause is a group of words including a subject and a verb conjugated in a specific tense. For example, *"We went to visit his parents"* is a clause – which we commonly define as a sentence, even if it is not the most appropriate word to use.

Each clause includes **one verb** only – if we do not count auxiliary and modal verbs, of course. Two or more verbs correspond, then, to two or more clauses.

There are two kinds of clauses:

- **Main clauses.** Also called independent clauses, they are the "core" of our speech, clauses that make sense on their own, even when there is not another sentence following them.

  Example: *I live in a small city.* The clause is already complete and makes sense.

- **Dependent clauses.** In order to make sense, a dependent clause needs to depend on a main one. It can start with words like *though, who, because, but,* etc.

  Example: *If we handle the situation.* You can see that this clause needs a main one to be complete and to make sense.

Now we can start talking about the two different types of sentences:

- **Simple sentences**. These have one clause only, which, obviously, is going to be the main one, as it is the only clause that can be used on its own.

  Example: *They are on a boat.*

- **Compound sentences**. These include more than just a clause. You will have a main clause and one or more dependent clauses having the same importance. The clauses can be joined with simple punctuation, coordinating conjunctions – *and, or, but, for,* etc. – and correlative ones – *not only… but also…,* etc.

  Example: They are on a boat <u>and</u> we will meet them at the port.

- **Complex sentences**. These include more than just a clause. You will have a main clause and one or more dependent clauses, but they are not on the same level, meaning that they can be joined with subordinate conjunctions like *because, however, although, even if...*

  Example: *They are on a boat <u>because</u> they like to sail.*

Examples:

- *I can come at 3 p.m. when my friends pick me up.*

This is a complex sentence because it has two verbs – can come and pick up. Remember that modal verbs are not counted as separate verbs. Now let's divide the two clauses: *I can come at 3 p.m. / when my friends pick me up.* The main clause is "I can come at 3 p.m.", as the sentence could stop after "p.m." and stand on its own. "When my friends pick me up" is a dependent clause, because it needs a main clause to make sense, and it's introduced by a subordinate conjunction.

- *We went to the party and had lots of fun.*

This is a compound sentence including two clauses (see the two verbs, *to go* and *to have*) linked by a coordinate conjunction (and). The main clause is "We went to the party", while the dependent one is "and had *lots of* fun".

We can see that, in English, the structure of a clause is – most of the time – quite regular. You would start the sentence with the subject pronoun followed by the conjugated verb and the other direct or indirect objects. Let's see how it works in Italian.

First of all, what we have seen for English clauses/sentences applies in Italian as well. We have **frasi principali** – the main clauses – **frasi coordinate** – the clauses introduced by a coordinate conjunction – and **frasi subordinate** – introduced by a subordinate conjunction. The combination of **frase principale** and one or more **frasi coordinate/subordinate** is called **periodo**.

In order to help you recognize them, and expand your vocabulary, in the following table you will find the main **congiunzioni coordinanti e subordinanti** – coordinate and subordinate conjunctions.

CONGIUNZIONI COORDINANTI coordinate conjunctions		CONGIUNZIONI SUBORDINANTI subordinate conjunctions	
e	and	**perché**	because
o/oppure	or	**mentre**	while
ma	but	**quando**	when
infatti	in fact	**come**	such as
quindi	so, therefore	**se**	if
cioè	that is	**prima/dopo che**	before/after
sia... sia	both... and	**nonostante**	despite
né... né	neither... nor	**che**	that/which

Examples:

- **Siamo andati al mare e abbiamo visitato la città.** *We went to the seaside and visited the city.* The coordinate conjuction is "e".

- **Marco si è arrabbiato perché il suo amico era in ritardo.** *Marco got angry because his friend was late.* The subordinate conjunction is "perché".

- **Prima che partissi, era molto preoccupata.** *Before you left, she was very worried.*

Let's take a closer look at the examples above. If we take into account the first example, we can see that the two clauses – the main sentence and the dependent one – are on the same level. How? If we switch them, the meaning is still the same. In fact, if we say **"Abbiamo visitato la città e siamo andati al mare"**, the main clause is now **"Abbiamo visitato la città"**, but the meaning of this compound sentence is unchanged.

Moving to the second example, here we have a complex sentence, as the dependant clause is introduced by a subordinate conjunction. In this instance, the main clause and the dependant one are **not** on the same level. We can prove it if we try to transform the dependant clause into the main one, as we have done for the first example. The sentence **"Il suo amico era in ritardo perché Marco si è arrabbiato"** – *His friend was late because Marco got angry* – does not have the same meaning as the original one.

Third example. We have another complex sentence, where the dependent clause is introduced by **"Prima che".** What we wanted to highlight here is that, sometimes, dependent clauses can **precede** the main ones, especially in Italian. In this instance, we could also say **"Era molto preoccupata prima che partissi"** and the meaning of the sentence would still be the same.

For the structure of a clause, in general, Italian sentences would start with the conjugated verb. If you remember, we have already said that subject pronouns are not commonly used in Italian. Reading a clause starting with a verb right away can be confusing at first, especially when you come from a language needing the subject pronouns to be explained – as in English, or even French – but once you learn the verb conjugation you will easily get used to it.

After the verb, as in English, you will find the direct and/or indirect objects, and then a coordinate or subordinate conjunction if it is a compound or complex sentence, respectively.

A WARNING

Italian sentences can be VERY long. Do not be scared if you are not able to spot a full stop between the lines of a text – it is completely normal. Also, if you receive a long text, you do not have to worry: it is not necessarily something important and serious. It can just be an excited friend telling you what happened to him/her the day before!

 **EXERCISES VI**

1) Frase principale, coordinata o subordinata? *Identify the following clauses. Are they main clauses (M), coordinate clauses (C) or subordinate (S) clauses?*

Example:

oppure ci incontriamo domani   (C)   *or we meet tomorrow*

E poi sono uscita	_____	*And then I went out*
La vita è bella	_____	*Life is beautiful*
Perché non volevo	_____	*Because I did not want to*
Quindi non sono partiti	_____	*So they did not leave*
Hai visto i suoi amici	_____	*You saw his friends*
Quando non lo sapevo	_____	*When I did not know it*
Ma ci penserò poi	_____	*But I will think about it later*
Il cane dorme sul divano	_____	*The dog sleeps on the couch*

2) Sottolinea i verbi nel testo e dividi le frasi. *Underline the verbs in the following text and divide the sentences with a slash (/).*

Example: <u>Vanno</u> sempre allo stesso ristorante / perché <u>è</u> buono ed economico.

Quando ero una bambina pensavo sempre al futuro. Il mio sogno era semplice: volevo diventare una pilota di aerei perché anche mio padre lo era. Nella mia camera tenevo tantissime miniature di aerei, che erano la mia più grande passione. Avevo anche altri sogni, però, come accogliere tanti animali in casa mia e occuparmi di loro. Se avessi avuto il tempo, avrei voluto anche imparare una nuova lingua.

Translation:

When I was a child, I was always thinking about the future. My dream was to become a pilot because my father was one. In my room, I had plenty of models of airplanes, which were my biggest passion. I also had other dreams, though, like sheltering many animals in my house and taking care of them. If I had had the time, I would have liked to learn a new language too.

UNIT 2

PRESENT TENSES

CHAPTER 1
THE PRESENT TENSE

Let's start our journey through verb conjugation with the present tense, which is commonly used on a daily basis to discuss current facts, habits, situations or events. Sometimes, it can also be used to talk about the future when it comes to scheduled activities.

Examples:

- *She has a sister.* (current situation)

- *The meeting ends at 5 p.m.* (future event)

In this chapter, we will focus on the simple present only, as we will dedicate another chapter of this section to the present continuous – the tense in a clause like *"I am driving to the restaurant"*, for example.

In English, the group of present tenses includes the present perfect too – for example, *"They have traveled across Europe"* – which expresses an action or a situation between past and present. In Italian, the present perfect does not exist as a tense, and this is why Italians struggle when they first learn it in school, as they do not understand when to use it. When it comes to actions started in the past – even if they still go on in the present – they just use the past tense.

In Italian, the simple present is called **presente semplice,** and it is used in the same way you would use it in English.

Before showing you how to conjugate a regular verb in the present tense, let's have a look at the conjugation of two of the most important – and most used – irregular verbs. *To be* and *to have,* **essere** e **avere**. Learning the conjugation of these two verbs is very important because – as we have already mentioned – you can use them alone or as auxiliary verbs, so you need them for both present and past tenses.

SOGGETTO *subject pronoun*	ESSERE *to be*	AVERE *to have*
io *I*	**sono** *am*	**ho** *have*
tu *you*	**sei** *are*	**hai** *have*
lui/lei/Lei *he/she/formal*	**è** *is*	**ha** *has*
noi *we*	**siamo** *are*	**abbiamo** *have*
voi *you*	**siete** *are*	**avete** *have*
loro *they*	**sono** *are*	**hanno** *have*

Before focusing on the conjugation of the verbs, let's take a closer look at the subject pronouns. The most striking difference that you might have noticed compared to the English language is that there is no *"it"* as a subject. The issue is easily solved: for objects and animals, you will just have to use *"he"* or *"she"* according to the gender of the animal or the noun of a specific object. In fact, all nouns are either masculine or feminine in Italian.

What about that formal **"Lei",** then? Well, in Italian, when you talk to someone that you do not know, someone who is older than you are, or is in a higher position than you – for example, your boss – it is important to **dare del Lei.** It literally means *"to give the she",* so referring to the other person using the subject pronoun *"she"* – the implication is that you will have to conjugate the verb according to that subject pronoun as well. Please note that the subject pronoun to use will be *"she",* no matter the gender of the person you are talking to.

We know that it might seem weird, but it is an important aspect of Italian culture. Some people can take offense if you talk to them using the subject pronoun *"you"* in those situations. Then, of course, it all depends on the person right in front of you. It often happens that, as soon as you talk to someone in a formal way, they will tell you **"Dammi del tu!",** which is their "permission" to start using the **"tu"** as a subject pronoun.

Examples:

- **Ciao Maria, hai visto le mie chiamate?**   *Hi Maria, did you see my calls?*

In this instance, we are using "tu" as a subject pronoun as we are talking to someone that we are already familiar with. Also, please note that in this clause the verb to have is used as an auxiliary.

- **Professore, è mai stato in Inghilterra?** *Professor, have you ever been to England?*

In this instance, we are using "Lei" as a subject pronoun as we are talking to a professor, someone who is in a higher position than you if you are still a student. Here, as in the previous example, the verb *to be* is used as an auxiliary verb.

Now that we know the conjugation of the verbs **essere** and **avere**, it is time to tackle the conjugation of regular verbs! In order to conjugate a regular verb, the very first thing to do is identifying the verb root – the part of the verb without the **-are, -ere, -ire** ending – and then attach the endings related to the present tense. Those endings are slightly different for each group, as you will see in the table below.

As examples, we will use the regular verbs **parlare, cadere** and **sentire** and we will conjugate them in the present tense. If we remove the endings related to the infinitive form of these verbs, we find out that the verb roots are **parl-, cad-** and **sent-**, respectively. The verb root never changes; the only thing that changes while conjugating the verb is the ending as it corresponds to the different subject pronoun.

SOGGETTO *subject pronoun*	PARLARE *to speak*	CADERE *to fall*	SENTIRE *to hear*
io *I*	**parl-o** *speak*	**cad-o** *fall*	**sent-o** *hear*
tu *you*	**parl-i** *speak*	**cad-i** *fall*	**sent-i** *hear*
lui/lei/Lei *he/she/formal*	**parl-a** *speaks*	**cad-e** *falls*	**sent-e** *hears*
noi *we*	**parl-iamo** *speak*	**cad-iamo** *fall*	**sent-iamo** *hear*
voi *you*	**parl-ate** *speak*	**cad-ete** *fall*	**sent-ite** *hear*
loro *they*	**parl-ano** *speak*	**cad-ono** *fall*	**sent-ono** *hear*

Let's take a closer look. First of all, you might have realized that – once again – the English language has spoiled us. In fact, in English, the verb barely changes when we have to conjugate it. The only thing that needs to be remembered is to add the ending **-s** when the subject pronouns are *he, she, it.* And this is also a reason why Italian speakers absolutely love English conjugation, as it is definitely easier to remember than the Italian one.

As the verb is almost always the same, in English we have to specify the subject pronoun while talking. In fact, if I say only *talk,* the corresponding subject pronouns could be *I, you, we, you, they.* In Italian, as the conjugated verb is always different, there is no need to specify the subject pronoun. If we take a look at the table above, you can see that if we say **parlano,** the only subject pronoun could be **loro,** they.

Beware! If you want to specify that the subject pronoun of a certain sentence is *I,* and you are writing it, **io** does not need a capital letter, unless it is at the beginning of a sentence.

As expected, the endings are not all different for each verb group. For example, the ending **-o** for the subject pronoun **io** is the same for the three groups of verbs. Same for **noi**, whose verb ending is always **-iamo**.

Some of the endings are the same for two of the three verb groups, especially for the **-ere** and **-ire** ones. We can see this if we take a look at the endings related to the subject pronouns **tu, lui/lei** and **loro**.

Below you will find some examples of sentences in the present tense:

Examples:

- **Ho 30 anni.**   *I am 30 years old.*

Beware! In Italian, to tell your age, you must use the verb *to have*, and not the verb *to be*.

- **Parla inglese e italiano**.   *He/She speaks English and Italian.*

Languages do not need a capital letter in Italian.

- **Siamo americani.**   *We are American.*

- **Americani** is the plural form of the masculine singular adjective **americano**. If our group was made of women only, we would say **siamo americane**.

Unfortunately, in Italian there are also a few irregular verbs – **i verbi irregolari**. Some of them share a similar conjugation, but for the others, the only thing you can do is learn them by heart, as they do not follow any specific rules. But do not worry! There are not too many. Our advice is to learn them little by little, even one per day. You will see that it will be easier to remember those verbs when you learn them in small doses. Flash cards are always a great help.

In the following tables, you will see the conjugation of the most used ones.

SOGGETTO	ANDARE *to go*	VENIRE *to come*	STARE *to stay*
io	vado	vengo	sto
tu	vai	vieni	stai
lui/lei/Lei	va	viene	sta
noi	andiamo	veniamo	stiamo
voi	andate	venite	state
loro	vanno	vengono	stanno

SOGGETTO	FARE *to do*	DARE *to give*	DIRE *to say*
io	faccio	do	dico
tu	fai	dai	dici
lui/lei/Lei	fa	dà	dice
noi	facciamo	diamo	diciamo
voi	fate	date	dite
loro	fanno	danno	dicono

SOGGETTO	USCIRE *to go out*	TENERE *to keep*	SCEGLIERE *to choose*
io	esco	tengo	scelgo
tu	esci	tieni	scegli
lui/lei/Lei	esce	tiene	sceglie
noi	usciamo	teniamo	scegliamo
voi	uscite	tenete	scegliete
loro	escono	tengono	scelgono

SOGGETTO	SALIRE *to go up*	RIUSCIRE *to manage to do something*	BERE *to drink*
io	salgo	riesco	bevo
tu	sali	riesci	bevi
lui/lei/Lei	sale	riesce	beve
noi	saliamo	riusciamo	beviamo
voi	salite	riuscite	bevete
loro	salgono	riescono	bevono

SOGGETTO	POTERE *to be able to – can*	SAPERE *to know*	VOLERE *to want*
io	posso	so	voglio
tu	puoi	sai	vuoi
lui/lei/Lei	può	sa	vuole
noi	possiamo	sappiamo	vogliamo
voi	potete	sapete	volete
loro	possono	sanno	vogliono

Now, are you ready to practice the verbs, and learn some useful vocabulary with our usual exercise session? **Andiamo!** *Let's go!*

📑 EXERCISES I

1) Completa la tabella. *Complete the table below with the conjugation of the verbs to have and to be*

SOGGETTO	AVERE	ESSERE
io		
tu		
lui/lei/Lei		
noi		
voi		
loro		

2) Coniuga i seguenti verbi al presente. *Conjugate the following verbs in the present tense Beware! There are both regular and irregular verbs.*

Example: They create ___creano___ **(creare)**

I think _____ (pensare)

We do _____ (fare)

She eats _____ (mangiare)

You drink _____ (bere, tu)

He discovers _____ (scoprire)

I go _____ (andare)

You choose _____ (scegliere, voi)

They sleep _____ (dormire)

3) Ascolta l'audio. *Listen to the audio and add the missing verbs in the present tense.*

_____ Francesca, _____ a Roma e _____ 35 anni.

Questa _____ la mia famiglia! _____ due genitori magnifici, Laura e Marco.

I miei fratelli, Luca e Paolo, _____ come camerieri in un ristorante famoso.

Nel mio tempo libero, _____ sport due volte alla settimana e _____ al cinema

il venerdì sera. Il sabato e la domenica _____ con i miei amici e a volte _____

gente nuova. _____ conoscere persone straniere, perché _____ nuove

culture e tradizioni, e _____ migliorare il mio inglese!

Translation:

I am Francesca, I live in Rome and I am 35 years old. This is my family! I have two amazing parents, Laura and Marco. My brothers, Luca and Paolo, work as waiters in a famous restaurant. In my free time, I play sports twice a week and I go the movies on Friday night. On Saturdays and Sundays, I go out with my friends and sometimes I meet new people. I love meeting foreigners because I discover new cultures and traditions, and I can improve my English!

CHAPTER 2
THE PRESENT TENSE OF REFLEXIVE VERBS

We talked about reflexive verbs in the first unit, explaining what they are, how you can recognize them, and what they look like. Now it is time to explore their conjugation in the present tense!

Do not worry: reflexive verbs do not have a completely different conjugation compared to what we have seen in the previous chapter. On the contrary, they are the same, but these verbs need something more: the reflexive pronoun, **il pronome riflessivo.**

Of course, when talking or writing, there is a huge difference if we say *You wash* or *You wash yourself.* In the first example, the object of the action can be anything: *the car, the dog, the floor,* etc. In the second one, we have the reflexive pronoun, so *you* are the subject and the object of that action. This is why we should never forget to add the reflexive pronouns when using a reflexive verb.

We have already shown the different reflexive pronouns, so how can you conjugate a reflexive verb? First of all, **repetita iuvant** – a Latin motto meaning that repeating does good. At their base form, all reflexive and reciprocal verbs are just like regular ones, meaning that they belong to the **-are, -ere, -ire** groups, but they end with the suffix **-si** instead.

Examples:

- **Vestirsi = vestire+si** *to get dressed*
- **Capirsi = capire+si** *to understand each other*

The only thing you have to do, then, is conjugate the verb according to its group, just as you have learned in the previous chapter. However, you must not forget to add the reflexive pronoun <u>before</u> the conjugated verb itself. Let's see a few examples:

SOGGETTO	SVEGLIARSI *to wake up*	METTERSI *to put on*	PENTIRSI *to regret*
io	mi sveglio	mi metto	mi pento
tu	ti svegli	ti metti	ti penti
lui/lei/Lei	si sveglia	si mette	si pente
noi	ci svegliamo	ci mettiamo	ci pentiamo
voi	vi svegliate	vi mettete	vi pentite
loro	si svegliano	si mettono	si pentono

The three reflexive verbs in the table above belong to the three different groups: **svegliarsi** is an **-are** verb, **mettersi** belongs to the **-ere** group, and **pentirsi** to the **-ire** one. As you can see, the only difference from the regular conjugation is the addition of the reflexive pronouns. The verb endings are the same. Easy, right?

In order to learn some useful vocabulary too, let's take a look at the description of a morning routine filled with reflexive verbs!

La mattina mi sveglio alle 8, ma non mi alzo mai prima delle 8:30. Poi vado in bagno e mi faccio una doccia. In inverno mi asciugo sempre i capelli mentre mia sorella si trucca. Mi vesto per la scuola mentre i miei genitori si preparano la colazione in cucina. Dopo aver mangiato, mi metto il cappotto e sono pronto a partire!

In the morning, I wake up at 8, but I never get up before 8:30. Then I go to the bathroom and take a shower. In winter, I always dry my hair while my sister puts her makeup on. I get dressed while my parents make their breakfast in the kitchen. After having eaten, I put my coat on and I am ready to leave!

Addormentarsi	*Radersi*	*Asciugarsi*	*Divertirsi*	*Laurearsi*	*Alzarsi*
Lavarsi	*Riposarsi*	*Tagliarsi*	*Tuffarsi*	*Bagnarsi*	*Ubriacarsi*
Svegliarsi	*Sdraiarsi*	*Pettinarsi*	*Vestirsi*	*Arrabbiarsi*	*Allenarsi*
Rilassarsi	*Guardarsi*	*Truccarsi*	*Travestirsi*	*Annoiarsi*	*Nascondersi*

📰 EXERCISES II

1) Sottolinea i verbi riflessivi. *Underline the reflexive verbs in the text.*

La mattina mi sveglio alle 8, ma non mi alzo mai prima delle 8:30. Poi vado in bagno e mi faccio una doccia. In inverno mi asciugo sempre i capelli mentre mia sorella si trucca. Mi vesto per la scuola mentre i miei genitori si preparano la colazione in cucina. Dopo aver mangiato, mi metto il cappotto e sono pronto a partire!

2) Coniuga i seguenti verbi riflessivi. *Conjugate the reflexive verbs in the table in the present tense.*

SOGGETTO	PETTINARSI *to comb your hair*	ALZARSI *to get up*
io		
tu		
lui/lei/Lei		
noi		
voi		
loro		

3) Parla della tua routine mattutina. *Taking inspiration from the text above, write a short text about your morning routine.*

_____

_____

_____

_____

CHAPTER 3
THE PRESENT CONTINUOUS

Now that we are talking about the present tense, we must also discuss the *present continuous!* In English, we use the present continuous to talk about actions in progress and to describe specific events happening in the present or in the future. For example, right now, *you are reading* this chapter. *You are reading* is a perfect example of the use of the present continuous to describe an action in progress.

Examples:

- *I am learning Italian.* (present)
- *They are leaving tomorrow at 5.* (future)

In Italian, there is a present continuous too, but its use and construction differ from the English one. First of all, the Italian present continuous is used to describe an event happening in the <u>present only</u>. You cannot use it to talk about future events – for those, you will have to use the future tense, which we will introduce in Unit 4.

In English, the present continuous is made of the verb *to be,* conjugated in the present tense, and the *-ing* form of the main verb. In Italian, the verb *to be* is replaced by the verb *to stay* – **stare** – conjugated in the present tense. Also, in Italian an *-ing* ending like the English one does not exist. In order to complete the present continuous, you have to use another tense – the so-called **gerundio.** In short, this is the construction of this tense in Italian:

(subject) + verb **stare** *conjugated* + **gerundio** *of the main verb*

We have already come across the conjugation of the verb **stare** in a previous chapter, while discussing the irregular verbs, but let's refresh our memory:

SOGGETTO	STARE *to stay*
io	sto
tu	stai
lui/lei/Lei	sta
noi	stiamo
voi	state
loro	stanno

Now, what is this **gerundio** tense? Do not be scared: it is actually one of the easiest tenses!

The first thing to do, as usual, is identify the verb root of the main verb. Then we have to add the corresponding ending of the gerundio tense. Yes, there is just one ending for each verb group, and it never changes! The only element you will have to conjugate is the verb **stare,** as the gerundio is invariable.

Here are the three endings of the **gerundio:**

- **-ando** for the **-are** verbs. The gerundio of the verb **parlare,** for example, is **parl-ando.**

- **-endo** for the **-ere** verbs. The gerundio of the verb **prendere,** for example, is **prend-endo.**

- **-endo** for the **-ire** verbs. The gerundio of the verb **capire,** for example, is **cap-endo.**

As you might have noticed, the ending for the **-ere** and **-ire** verbs is actually the same.

Examples:

- **Sto guidando il bus.**   *I am driving the bus.*

Guidando is the gerundio tense of the verb **guidare,** *to drive.* Its verb root is **guid-** and the ending of the verb group is **-ando**. The definite article used for the bus is **il,** as the word *bus* is a masculine singular one in Italian.

- **Sta vincendo la gara.**   *She/He is winning the competition.*

Vincendo is the gerundio tense of the verb **vincere,** *to win.* Its verb root is **vinc-** and the ending of the verb group is **-endo**. The definite article used for the competition is **la,** as the word *competition* is a feminine singular one in Italian.

- **Stanno venendo a casa.**   *They are coming home.*

Venendo is the gerundio tense of the verb **venire,** *to come.* Its verb root is **ven-** and the ending of the verb group is **-endo**. Please note that, in Italian, the word *home* needs a preposition when there is movement towards it, as in this instance. The Italian preposition you have to use is **a,** which corresponds to the English *to.*

Well, that is all you have to know about the Italian present continuous. Now let's practice!

📑 EXERCISES III

1) Traduci le seguenti frasi. *Translate the following clauses using the present continuous.*

Example: She is crying <u>sta piangendo</u> **(piangere)**

- They are watching _____ (guardare)

- He is studying _____ (studiare)

- I am leaving _____ (partire)

- You are eating _____ (mangiare, tu)

- You are paying _____ (pagare, voi)

- We are dancing _____ (ballare)

- I am cooking _____ (cucinare)

2) Quale tempo verbale? *Read the following sentences in English and write whether you should use the future (F) or the present continuous (PC) in Italian.*

- Next week I am going to the beach. _____

- I am studying Italian for my exam. _____

- They are going home this weekend. _____

- She is getting dressed for tonight's party. _____

- You are picking up the kids at 4 p.m. _____

- Sandra is planning her next holiday. _____

- My cousins are visiting Paris. _____

3) Che cosa stai facendo? *What are you doing right now? Answer the question in Italian.*

_____

_____

_____

_____

_____

_____

CHAPTER 4
THE IMPERATIVE MOOD

Start studying the imperative mood in Italian!

Well, that was a good example of the imperative mood in English. In fact, this mood is used for direct commands and requests, but using the imperative mood does not mean being impolite!

There are different situations requiring the use of this tense:

- **Positive commands:** *Please walk the dog; Finish your homework before going out; Turn off the TV if you are not watching;* etc.

- **Negative commands:** *Do not smoke in here; Do not be late for school; Please do not call me in the afternoon;* etc.

- **Commands involving yourself:** *Let's go to the party; Let's plan our next holidays before March; Let's buy some new clothes;* etc.

One of the main features of its construction is the absence of the subject pronoun. The clause, then, typically start with an invariable verb. Well, in Italian, the imperative mood is a little bit more complicated. Let's say that there are more things to take into account. First of all, good news: the use of the imperative mood is the same as in English!

However, you will have to conjugate the verb. And yes, you will have to conjugate it in the present tense, but you have the following options:

- Conjugating the verb according to the subject pronoun *you*, singular. **Beware!** If you are using a verb belonging to the **-are** group, the verb ending will not be **-i,** as we saw when discussing the simple present, but **-a.**

  Examples: Apri la finestra! *Open the window!*

  Pensa a tua moglie! *Think about your wife!*

- Conjugating the verb according to the subject pronoun *she* to use the courtesy form, when talking with someone you do not know, someone who is older than you or is in a higher position. In this instance, though, the tense to use is not the simple present, but the present subjunctive, that we will introduce in the final unit of this book. The same applies to the subject pronoun *they.*

Example: Usi quella penna per scrivere, *Use that pen to write, please.*

- Conjugating the verb according to the subject pronoun *we*. This form corresponds to the English one using *Let's...*

Example: Facciamo una pausa! *Let's take a break!*

- Conjugating the verb according to the subject pronoun *you*, plural.

Example: Per favore prendete lo scontrino con voi! *Please take the receipt with you!*

In the table below, you will see a few examples of some verb conjugation in the imperative mood.

SOGGETTO	CANTARE *to sing*	PRENDERE *to take*	FINIRE *to finish*
tu	canta!	prendi!	finisci!
Lei	canti!	prenda!	finisca!
noi	cantiamo!	prendiamo!	finiamo!
voi	cantate!	prendete!	finite!
loro	cantino!	prendano!	finiscano!

As for negative commands, the only thing you have to do is add a **non** in front of the verb, as we have already seen while discussing the present tense. Also, the verb must be in its infinitive form when the subject pronoun is *you*, singular, but it needs to be conjugated with all the other subject pronouns.

Examples:

- **Non parlare!**   *Don't speak!*

- **Non scrivete quel messaggio, per favore.**   *Don't write that text, please.*

Now, what happens when we want to conjugate a reflexive verb in the imperative mood? Well, in this instance, as weird as it might seem, the reflexive pronoun will be attached at the end of the verb. For example, **ti metti i tuoi jeans** means *you put your jeans on,* and it is a simple clause in the present tense. If we transform the verb in the imperative mood, the clause will become **mettiti i tuoi jeans!** The reflexive pronoun **ti** is now attached to the conjugated verb **metti**.

The above does <u>not</u> apply when conjugating the imperative mood according to the subject pronouns **Lei** and **loro** as, in those instances, we have to use the subjunctive tense, as already explained above.

Before closing this chapter, let's look at the conjugation of a couple of reflexive verbs in the imperative mood.

SOGGETTO	ALZARSI *to get up*	VESTIRSI *to get dressed*
tu	alzati!	vestiti!
Lei	si alzi!	si vesta!
noi	alziamoci!	vestiamoci!
voi	alzatevi!	vestitevi!
loro	si alzino!	si vestano!

 **EXERCISES IV**

1) Scrivi la coniugazione dei verbi all'imperativo. *Write the conjugation of the following verbs in the imperative mood.*

SOGGETTO	BALLARE *to dance*	MUOVERSI *to hurry*	VINCERE *to win*
tu			
Lei			
noi			
voi			
loro			

2) Scrivi l'ordine/la richiesta corrispondente alla situazione. *Write the command/ request according to the context using the imperative mood.*

Example: He is in a restaurant _____**non fumare**_____ **(fumare, to smoke)**

· He is in the classroom _____ (parlare, to speak)

· We are on the beach _____ (nuotare, to swim)

· You are running a marathon _____ (correre, to run)

· He is trying to learn Italian _____ (studiare, to study)

· You want to stay fit _____ (allenarsi, to work out)

· He is lying _____ (mentire, to lie)

UNIT 3

PAST TENSES

CHAPTER 1
THE SIMPLE PAST

With this new Unit, we will focus on Italian past tenses. We are using the plural because – as in English – there are several past tenses. Actually, as you might suspect, the Italian language has more past tenses than English does. But do not worry: they are not difficult, and you will find several similarities with English past tenses.

The first one we will discuss is the simple past, the tense we use to talk about actions or events started and ended in the past. In fact, the emphasis is on the fact that the action is <u>finished</u>. In English, the simple past of regular verbs is made by adding the ending -*ed* to the verb root.

Examples:

- *Yesterday I played with the dog in the park.*

- *Two years ago, I visited the MoMA for the first time.*

Of course, in English, there are **a lot** of irregular verbs. In those cases, unfortunately, the only thing you can do is learn them by heart, which is kind of a nightmare for Italian speakers.

In Italian, the tense we use to talk about past actions and events which started and ended in the past is the so-called **passato prossimo**. Good news: you are already familiar with its structure!

How is that possible? Well, the structure of the **passato prossimo** resembles that of the <u>present perfect</u> tense – the tense in a sentence like *I have traveled all over the world,* for example. The structure of the present perfect is the following one:

Subject pronoun + to have + past participle of the main verb

Well, this is the structure of the **passato prossimo:**

(subject) + auxiliary verb (to be/to have) + past participle of the main verb

In order to use this tense, you have to know how to form the past participle of a verb in Italian. As in English, there are regular and irregular past participles, but – for once – there are more irregular ones in English than in Italian!

As for the regular past participles, they are very easy to form. Once again, we have to take the verb root and attach the ending corresponding to the verb group.

Specifically:

- For **-are** verbs, the ending of the past participle is **-ato**.
  Examples: mangiare-mangiato, parlare-parlato, cantare-cantato, etc.

- For **-ere** verbs, the ending of the past participle is **-uto**.
  Examples: cadere-caduto, avere-avuto, credere-creduto, etc.

- For **-ire** verbs, the ending of the past participle is **-ito**.
  Examples: sentire-sentito, capire-capito, partire-partito, etc.

Beware! Please note that irregular verbs in the present tense can have a regular past participle. If we look at the examples above, we can see that the verbs **avere** and **capire have a regular past participle, despite having** an irregular conjugation in the present tense.

You will find a list with the most common irregular past participles at the end of this book. Our advice is to learn them little by little, but **regularly**. For example, we would suggest learning two or three of them per day, every day. It will only take you a few minutes, but that way you will not feel overwhelmed, and you will feel more confident when using them.

Now, if we take into account the structure of the passato prossimo presented above, the next question is: *how do I know when I have to use the verb to have or to be as the auxiliary?*

The vast majority of verbs require **avere** as the auxiliary. Let's look at the conjugation in the simple past of three verbs requiring the auxiliary *to have,* each one belonging to a different verb group. Please note that the verb **bere** has an irregular past participle.

SOGGETTO	MANGIARE *to eat*	BERE *to drink*	PULIRE *to clean*
io	ho mangiato	ho bevuto	ho pulito
tu	hai mangiato	hai bevuto	hai pulito
lui/lei/Lei	ha mangiato	ha bevuto	ha pulito
noi	abbiamo mangiato	abbiamo bevuto	abbiamo pulito
voi	avete mangiato	avete bevuto	avete pulito
loro	hanno mangiato	hanno bevuto	hanno pulito

As you might have noticed, when using the auxiliary *to have,* the past participle is <u>invariable</u>. It is always the same: the only thing you will have to conjugate is the verb *to have* in the present tense.

Examples:

- **Ha cucinato un piatto ottimo.** *He/She cooked a delicious meal.*

- **Ho preso l'autobus ieri**. *I took the bus yesterday.*

Please note that the verb **prendere** – to take – has an irregular past participle, **preso**.

On the other hand, you will have to use **essere** as the auxiliary verb for:

- Verbs of movement.

  Example: sono andato, *I went.*

- The verb *to be* itself.

  Example: sei stato, *you were.*

- Verbs suggesting a change regarding the subject, such as growing up, getting old, becoming something/someone, being born, dying, etc.

  Example: sono cresciuti, *they grew up.*

- Reflexive and reciprocal verbs.

  Example: ci siamo baciati, *we kissed.*

- Verbs in the passive voice. Please note that the passive voice is used more commonly in Italian than in English. More about it in the fourth chapter of this unit.

  Example: la riunione è stata spostata, *the meeting has been rescheduled.*

- Impersonal verbs, which are verbs not referring to a real person, thing or animal doing the action. In English, impersonal verbs are introduced by the subject pronoun *it.*

  Example: mi è sembrato difficile, *it seemed difficult to me.*

In the following table, you will see the conjugation of three verbs in the simple past requiring the auxiliary *to be*. Please note that the last verb – **pentirsi** – is a reflexive one.

SOGGETTO	INVECCHIARE *to get old*	ESSERE *to be*	PENTIRSI *to regret*
io	sono invecchiato/a	sono stato/a	mi sono pentito/a
tu	sei invecchiato/a	sei stato/a	ti sei pentito/a
lui/lei/Lei	è invecchiato/a	è stato/a	si è pentito/a
noi	siamo invecchiati/e	siamo stati/e	ci siamo pentiti/e
voi	siete invecchiati/e	siete stati/e	vi siete pentiti/e
loro	sono invecchiati/e	sono stati/e	si sono pentiti/e

As you might have noticed, there is something happening regarding the past participle. In fact, when using the auxiliary *to be,* the past participle must match the gender and the number of the subject pronoun it refers to. It behaves like an adjective, meaning that the past participle has four forms: two singular and two plural ones, each one having a masculine and a feminine form.

To explain it better, if we take the examples above, **invecchiato** – with an -o at the end – is a past participle in its masculine singular form. It means that the subject is a man, a male animal, or a masculine object. **Invecchiata**, instead, is a past participle in the feminine singular form. **Invecchiati** is the masculine plural form, and **invecchiate** is the feminine plural one.

When you need to use the auxiliary *to be,* then, you will have to conjugate the verb *to be,* and then remember to adapt the past participle according to the subject of your sentence. Do not forget to add the reflexive pronoun when needed, though!

Examples:

- **È partito alle 3.**   *He left at 3.*

- **Ci siamo vestite a casa mia.**   *We got dressed at my house.*

Please note the ending -*e* of the past participle. It suggests that the subject is a group of women only.

One last thing before finishing this chapter: here are a few useful words you might need when using the past tense.

ieri	*yesterday*
l'altroieri	*the day before yesterday (literally, the other yesterday)*
la settimana scorsa	*last week*
il mese scorso	*last month*
due giorni fa	*two days ago*

Please note that you need to adapt the word **scorso** to the gender and the number of the word it refers to. This is why you have **scorsa** – as **settimana** is a feminine singular noun – and **scorso** – as **mese** is a masculine singular noun.

📑 EXERCISES I

1) Essere o avere? *Do the following Italian verbs require to be or to have as the auxiliary for construction of the simple past? Put an X in the table below.*

	AVERE	ESSERE
CONTROLLARE *to check*		
ABBRACCIARSI *to hug each other*		
NASCERE *to be born*		
STIRARE *to iron*		
PARTIRE *to leave*		
ACCENDERE *to switch on*		

2) Scrivi il passato prossimo. *Write the simple past of the following verbs in Italian. Please note that some of them might have an irregular past participle. Use the list at the end of the book as a reference when in doubt.*

Example: I understood _____**ho capito**_____ **(capire)**

· They discovered _____ (scoprire)

· She was _____ (essere)

· I drove _____ (guidare)

· Giulia and Martina went _____ (andare)

· You saw _____ (vedere, tu)

- You saw each other   _____ (vedersi, voi)

- He was born   _____ (nascere)

- I watched   _____ (guardare)

3) Ascolta l'audio. *Listen to the audio file and add the missing verbs in the simple past.*

Ieri _____ una bella giornata. Io e mia sorella _____ in

città per andare a trovare un nostro amico. _____ la macchina perché ci

vogliono trenta minuti circa per arrivare da lui. Quando _____, Marco

_____ subito un buon caffè. _____ tutto il pomeriggio insieme e

_____ un film che _____ molto.

Translation:

Yesterday was a good day. My sister and I went to the city to visit a friend of ours. We took the car because it takes about thirty minutes to get to his place. When we arrived, Marco served us a good coffee right away. We spent all afternoon together and we watched a movie that we really liked.

CHAPTER 2
THE IMPERFECT TENSE

The imperfect tense – **l'imperfetto** – is the second most used tense to describe an action or an event that took place in the past. *Why is it different from the **passato prossimo,** then? When should we use one over the other?*

Even if in English the imperfect tense does not exist, the difference from the simple past is quite easy to understand. The imperfect has to be used when we are talking about a prolonged / ongoing action in the past. It is not a simple event which started and finished.

For example, when you are talking about your experiences at school, it is likely that you will have to use the imperfect tense, as you're describing events which used to happen on a regular basis, not just once. On the other hand, if you want to discuss a movie you watched last weekend, you will use the simple past, as you're describing something which happened only once, at a precise moment in time.

Here are a few situations that might require the imperfect tense:

- Continuous actions in the past.
- Conversations about feelings and emotions.
- Habits.

Also, you have to use the imperfect tense after the word **mentre**, *while.*

As for translating into English – considering that there is not a corresponding tense – you can use the simple past or the present perfect.

Looking forward to some good news?

Well, the **imperfetto** is probably the most regular tense ever. This is why all students love it. But beware! Even if the imperfect is one of the easiest Italian verb tenses, that does not mean you can use it all the time, while putting the **passato prossimo** aside!

In fact, the endings are almost the same for the three groups!

As you will see in the following table, the "signature" consonant of this tense is letter V, which is going to be repeated throughout the verb conjugation.

Take a look at the endings of the imperfect tense with the following conjugation of three verbs – one for each group. We have broken down the first conjugated verb in order to show you the two building blocks of this tense..

SOGGETTO	CAMMINARE *to walk*	VEDERE *to see*	DORMIRE *to sleep*
io	cammin-avo	ved-evo	dorm-ivo
tu	camminavi	vedevi	dormivi
lui/lei/Lei	camminava	vedeva	dormiva
noi	camminavamo	vedevamo	dormivamo
voi	camminavate	vedevate	dormivate
loro	camminavano	vedevano	dormivano

Easy, right? The only thing you have to remember is to add the right vowel according to the verb group, followed by the consonant *v*, and the endings shown above.

Of course, **non è tutto oro quel che luccica,** *not all that glitters is gold!*

There are a few irregular verbs. But do not worry, there are just a few of them. You will find the most used ones in the table below.

SOGGETTO	ESSERE *to be*	FARE *to do*	BERE *to drink*	DIRE *to say*
io	ero	facevo	bevevo	dicevo
tu	eri	facevi	bevevi	dicevi
lui/lei/Lei	era	faceva	beveva	diceva
noi	eravamo	facevamo	bevevamo	dicevamo
voi	eravate	facevate	bevevate	dicevate
loro	erano	facevano	bevevano	dicevano

Before starting to practice with some exercises, let's look at a few examples of sentences with the imperfect tense alone, or along with the simple past.

Examples:

- **Andavo sempre a scuola in bus.** *I always used to go to school by bus.*

- **Ci ha chiamato anche se era malata.** *She called us even if she was sick.*

- **Da adolescente mi piaceva andare in discoteca.** *I liked going to clubs as a teenager.*

📑 EXERCISES II

1) Imperfetto o passato prossimo? *Decide if you have to use the imperfect tense (I) or the simple past (SP) when translating the following sentences into Italian. Please note that there may be two verbs.*

- I was very shy at 18.   _____

- Yesterday they went to the cinema.   _____

- She came, even if she had a meeting.   _____   _____

- We ate a delicious pizza.   _____

- You traveled every weekend.   _____

- On Sundays, I slept until midday.   _____

- Did you meet Carlo this morning?   _____

2) Coniuga i verbi all'imperfetto. *Conjugate the following verbs in the imperfect tense.*

SOGGETTO	PARLARE *to talk*	CREDERE *to believe*	ESSERE *to be*	CUCIRE *to sew*
io				
tu				
lui/lei/Lei				
noi				
voi				
loro				

3) Ascolta l'audio. *Listen to the audio file and add the missing verbs in the simple past or imperfect tense.*

Quando _____ un bambino, _____ di diventare un medico perché

_____ il lavoro di mio padre. _____ sempre _____

aiutare gli altri e fare qualcosa che facesse la differenza. _____ per dieci

anni all'università per realizzare il mio sogno. _____ difficile, ma non

_____ mollare; _____ a letto tardissimo per studiare.

_____ l'anno scorso e adesso _____ a lavorare in ospedale.

Translation:

When I was a child, I dreamed about becoming a doctor because it was my father's job. I have always wanted to help others and do something that would make a difference. I have studied for ten years to make my dream come true. It has been hard, but I did not want to give up; I used to go to bed very late because I had to study. I graduated last year, and now I have started to work in the hospital.

CHAPTER 3
THE PAST PERFECT

Now we know the tenses used to talk about past actions or events. But what about actions or events that happened even before those events? That is when we have to use the past perfect tense.

We have to take into account the timeline of the events. For example, *I had finished my homework when my friend called me.* Here we have two verbs corresponding to two different clauses, joined by *when*. The first one is *I had finished my homework,* which is also the main clause, as it can stand on its own and makes perfect sense. The second clause – *when my friend called me* – is a dependent one, as it needs to depend on the main clause to make sense.

While in the main clause we have a verb in the past perfect – *I had finished* – in the dependent one we used the simple past – *my friend called.* Why, though? Because the timeline is the following: *I had finished my homework → my friend called.* It means that first, I had finished my homework (less recent event), and then my friend called (more recent event). Both events happened in the past. This is why we use the past perfect tense for the less recent one.

In terms of construction, the past perfect tense is made of:

Subject pronoun + simple past of the verb to have + past participle of the main verb

Good news! In Italian, there is a tense corresponding to the past perfect – **il trapassato prossimo.** And whenever you use the past perfect in English, you will have to use the **trapassato prossimo** in Italian. The rule is the same: this tense is needed when talking about an action/event that happened in the past before another one in the past.

Now, let's look at its construction:

(soggetto) + ausiliare (essere/avere) all'imperfetto + participio passato del verbo principale

In the following table, you will find the conjugation of two verbs in the past perfect tense.

You can see that the construction of past perfect in Italian is not that different from the English one. However, once again, there is no need to mention the subject pronoun, unless you really want to specify it.

SOGGETTO	PORTARE *to bring*	PARTIRE *to leave*
io	avevo portato	ero partito/a
tu	avevi portato	eri partito/a
lui/lei/Lei	aveva portato	era partito/a
noi	avevamo portato	eravamo partiti/e
voi	avevate portato	eravate partiti/e
loro	avevano portato	erano partiti/e

Also, as you might have noticed, when it comes to the auxiliary, you will have to choose between **essere** – *to be* – and **avere** – *to have*. How can you do it? Well, you will just have to choose the auxiliary based on the rules mentioned when discussing the simple past – **il passato prossimo**. If a verb needs the auxiliary *to be* for the simple past, it will need the same one for the past perfect.

Examples:

- **Ho mangiato**   *I ate*   **Avevo mangiato**   *I had eaten*
- **Siamo andati**   *We went*   **Eravamo andati**   *We had gone*

Beware! Please note that, in Italian, the auxiliary verb is not conjugated in the simple past but in the imperfect tense, the tense you studied in the previous chapter. Do not forget that *to be* is one of the few verbs with an irregular conjugation in the imperfect tense.

As for the past participle, do not forget to check whether the verb you want to use has an irregular one. Use the list at the end of this book for reference. If the verb has a regular past participle, you will have to apply the rules explained when discussing the simple past in the first chapter of this unit.

One last important thing: whenever you use *to be* as the auxiliary, you will have to choose the right form of the past participle according to the gender and the number of the subject it refers to. If the main verb requires the auxiliary *to have,* **nessun problema**, *no problem:* the past participle is invariable and does not change throughout the conjugation.

For negative sentences, as usual, the only thing you will have to do is add a **non** in front of the auxiliary verb.

Here are a few examples of sentences with useful vocabulary and verbs conjugated in the past perfect and other tenses.

Examples:

- **Aveva studiato molto per l'esame che poi ha superato.**
  She had studied a lot for the exam that she then passed.

In this example, we have a past perfect – **aveva studiato** – and a simple past – **ha superato**. The first clause requires the past perfect as the action – *studying* – precedes the event of passing the exam.

- **Sono tornati in Inghilterra anche se ci erano già stati.**
  They went back to England even though they had already been there.

In this example, the clause with the past perfect is the second one, and this is the timeline: *they had already been in England in the past → they went back there once again afterwards*. Please note that, as both verbs – **tornare** and **essere** – require *to be* as the auxiliary, the past participle had to be adapted to the masculine plural form according to the subject pronoun *they*.

📰 EXERCISES III

1) Coniuga i verbi al trapassato prossimo. *Conjugate the following verbs in the past perfect tense.*

SOGGETTO	VEDERE *to see*	CONCENTRARSI *to focus*	AGIRE *to act*
io			
tu			
lui/lei/Lei			
noi			
voi			
loro			

2) Rimetti insieme le parole nell'ordine giusto. *Put the following words in the right order to form sentences with the past perfect.*

Example: ricevuto / rimborso / ho / non / avevo / chiesto / mai / l'ho / un / ma

    Avevo chiesto un rimborso, ma non l'ho mai avuto

I had asked for a refund, but I never got it.

- il campanello / ero / il postino / quando / uscita / ha suonato / appena

I had just left when the postman rang the bell.

- quando / partiti / è / appena / sentito / erano / si / male

---

They had just left when he felt sick.

- invitato / cambiato / Luca e Marco / ma / idea / avevano / matrimonio / poi / hanno / al

---

They had invited Luca and Marco to the wedding, but then they changed their minds.

CHAPTER 4
THE REMOTE PAST TENSE

Wait... the remote what?

Well, yes, there is also a past tense which is called *remote past tense* – **il passato remoto,** in Italian. And there is a reason for its weird name.

Do you remember the simple past? The name of that tense is **passato prossimo,** which literally means *the near past.* In Italian, then, there is a near past and a remote past. What is the difference, though?

It is quite easy to understand. We use the first one to talk about more recent events in the past. Of course, the notion of "recent" when it comes to the past can be highly subjective. For example, for some people ten years ago can be a long time ago, while others can think otherwise.

Let's be honest. The remote past tense is not used very often in Italian. We mainly find it, for example, in books and newspaper articles, so it is not a tense you must know to be fluent in Italian.

However, since we designed this book to be a comprehensive guide to the Italian verb tenses, we had to mention it. Also, you might need this tense for reading purposes, for example if you want to read a book in Italian.

In short, we are talking about this tense so that you can recognize it when you cross paths with it, but learning its conjugation by heart is not really required to speak good Italian.

 FUN FACT: in some regions, such as Tuscany, the use of the **passato remoto** is quite widespread, even though it's used in the wrong way. People use this tense to talk about something that happened the year before, when they should use the **passato prossimo** instead.

Let's look at three verbs with a regular conjugation in this tense.

SOGGETTO	ANDARE *to go*	RICEVERE *to receive*	PARTIRE *to leave*
io	andai	ricevei *	partii
tu	andasti	ricevesti	partisti
lui/lei/Lei	andò	ricevé *	partì
noi	andammo	ricevemmo	partimmo
voi	andaste	riceveste	partiste
loro	andarono	riceverono *	partirono

* There are alternative endings for some **-ere** verbs conjugated in the 1ˢᵗ and 3ʳᵈ person singular (I/he/she), and in the 3ˢᵗ plural (they). The alternatives are **ricevetti, ricevette** and **ricevettero**, respectively.

Such a weird conjugation, isn't it? Do not worry, Italians think the same. It is probably the weirdest conjugation ever. Plus, this is the first time that we come across a few alternative endings, and just for one of the three verb groups!

This conjugation is kind of old-fashioned, and that is why it is not commonly used in everyday life. However, if you are a writer or a journalist and you are planning to write something in Italian, well, you have no choice: you must learn this tense!

Obviously, there are also some irregular verbs. In the following tables, you will find some examples of the most common ones. Once again, no need to learn them, just keep them in mind so that you can recognize them and understand what you are reading.

SOGGETTO	ESSERE *to be*	AVERE *to have*	FARE *to do/make*
io	fui	ebbi	feci
tu	fosti	avesti	facesti
lui/lei/Lei	fu	ebbe	fece
noi	fummo	avemmo	facemmo
voi	foste	aveste	faceste
loro	fossero	ebbero	fecero

SOGGETTO	DARE *to give*	SCRIVERE *to write*	DECIDERE *to decide*
io	diedi	scrissi	decisi
tu	desti	scrivesti	decidesti
lui/lei/Lei	diede/dette	scrisse	decise
noi	demmo	scrivemmo	decidemmo
voi	deste	scriveste	decideste
loro	diedero/dettero	scrissero	decisero

We know, it is hard. But once again, you are not obliged to learn it. It is always useful to know that this tense exists, though!

 FUN FACT: when it comes to the **passato remoto**, you'll understand the importance of accents in Italian! If you write **lavoro** – as in the conjugated verb, and not the noun *work* – the translation is *I work*. On the other hand, if you write **lavorò** – with the accent on the last vowel – you're actually writing *he/she worked,* with the verb conjugated in the remote past tense.

CHAPTER 5
THE PASSIVE VOICE

Before delving into the world of the passive voice, we should probably discuss what the active voice is. The active voice is when there is a clause whose subject performs the action expressed by the verb. For example, a simple clause like *Mary is eating an apple* shows the use of the active voice, where Mary is the one performing the action expressed by the verb – *eating an apple,* in this instance.

The passive voice is when the subject becomes the recipient of the verb's action. For example, *the mice are chased by the cat.* As you can see, the mice are suffering – by all means! – the action performed by the cat, and they are not the ones performing it directly. We could transform the clause into the active voice by saying *the cat chases the mice.*

If every passive voice has a corresponding active one, the same cannot be said for all active voices. Only transitive verbs have both. We invite you to take a look at the chapter about transitive and intransitive verbs to review the difference between them.

Let's look at some examples of sentences in the passive voice, along with the corresponding ones in the active voice.

Examples:

- *In 1789, the Bastille was stormed by the revolutionaries. (Passive voice)*

  The revolutionaries stormed the Bastille in 1789. (Active voice)

- *The floor has been cleaned. (Passive voice)*

  Someone has cleaned the floor. (Active voice)

- *A cake will be made by their friends. (Passive voice)*

  Their friends will make a cake. (Active voice)

As you can see from the examples above, in English, the subject performing the action is always introduced by the preposition *by* and you will find it at the end of the clause.

In the construction of the passive voice in English, what we have to do is use the verb *to be* in the appropriate tense and then add the past participle of the main verb. For example, if in an active clause we have a verb conjugated in the future tense, you will have to use the future of the verb *to be* and then add the past participle of the verb for the passive voice. In short, it is the main verb dictating the tense of the verb *to be* in the passive voice.

Now, let's start discussing the passive voice in Italian. For starters, the "rules" for the passive voice are the same, meaning that in a passive sentence the subject is acted upon.

Let's start with the easiest one – yeah, sorry to tell you that there is more than one.

The Italian passive voice works as in English, meaning that you will have to use the verb *to be* – **essere** – conjugated according to the tense you need + the past participle of the main verb. This is why we have introduced the passive voice at the end of this chapter. In order to build the passive voice, you need to know how to build a past participle.

Beware! As you will be using the verb *to be* as the auxiliary, do not forget to adapt the past participle according to the gender and number of the subject it refers to!

Let's look at a few examples with some of the tenses you have learned so far. For each sentence in the passive voice, we will also mark the corresponding clause in the active voice.

Examples:

- **La borsa è presa da mia sorella.**   *The bag is taken by my sister.*

    Mia sorella prende la borsa.   *My sister takes the bag.*

- **Il pesce è stato mangiato.**   *The fish has been eaten.*

    Qualcuno ha mangiato il pesce.   *Someone has eaten the fish.*

- **Giulio era stato colpito da lei.**   *Giulio was impressed by her.*

    Lei aveva colpito Giulio.   *She impressed Giulio.*

In the examples above, you have a passive voice with verbs in the present tense, simple past, and past perfect, respectively. Please note that, in the translations above, to make the sentence smoother in English, the tenses may not correspond with the original clause in Italian.

Now, an important thing to highlight. In English, the subject is introduced by the preposition *by* in the passive voice. In Italian, the subject performing the action in the active voice will be introduced by the preposition **da**, as you can see in the examples above.

However, when the preposition is followed by a definite article – as in *by the* – it will merge with **"da"**, forming an articulated preposition! In the table below, you will find the articulated preposition you might need when the preposition **"da"** is followed by one of the Italian definite articles.

DEFINITE ARTICLE	ARTICULATED PREPOSITION (*da*+definite article)
il *used in front of masculine singular nouns*	**dal**
lo *used in front of masculine singular nouns starting with the letters S+consonant, PS, PN, GN, X, Z, Y*	**dallo**
la *used for feminine singular nouns*	**dalla**
l' *used for singular nouns beginning with a vowel*	**dall'**
i *plural of **il***	**dai**
gli *plural of **lo** and **l'** for masculine nouns*	**dagli**
le *plural of **la** and **l'** for feminine nouns*	**dalle**

We know, the English language has spoiled us once again with just one definite article – *the* – whereas the Italian language has seven of them. *SEVEN!* However, we are introducing the definite articles now, so that you know the articulated prepositions you will need when using the passive voice in Italian.

Examples:

- **Il cane è stato preso <u>dalla</u> famiglia.**   *The dog was taken <u>by the</u> family.*

In this example you have the passive voice, as the subject performing the action is the family. The articulated preposition in Italian is **dalla,** as **famiglia** is a feminine singular noun, so it requires the definite article **la.**

- **La casa era stata pulita dall'ospite.**   *The apartment had been cleaned by the guest.*

In this example, we have a passive voice because the subject – *the guest* – and the object – *the apartment* – of an action – *cleaning* – have been reversed. The articulated preposition is **dall',** as **ospite** is masculine singular word beginning with a vowel. Please note that the past participle is in its feminine singular form – **pulita** – as it refers to the word **casa,** a feminine singular noun.

Now, the second option to build the passive voice in Italian requires the verb **venire**, *to come,* as weird as it might seem. That means, instead of the auxiliary *to be,* you will have to use and conjugate this other verb. As it is an irregular verb, we invite you to review its conjugation in the first unit.

Please note that you can use this construction for passive voice in the <u>present</u> and in the <u>future</u> tense only.

Examples:

- **La bambina viene data alla nonna.**   *The child is given to the grandmother.*
- **Verrà organizzata una grande festa.**   *A big party will be organized.*

Finally, one last option regarding the passive voice: the impersonal – the so-called **si passivante**. It is common in Italian, and it is used when the subject is a generic one or represents all of us, the people. For example, this construction can be used when discussing rules, customs, traditions, behaviors. Unfortunately, a similar construction does not exist in English, which makes the **si passivante** a little harder to explain and understand. We simply do not have a corresponding translation in English.

There is no actual subject in this kind of sentence. You will need the **si** and then the verb conjugated according to the tense you need.

Examples:

- **Non si fuma al ristorante.**   *You cannot smoke in the restaurant.*

- **In famiglia si litiga spesso.**   *Families often fight.*

- **Non si sono scoperti gli assassini.**   *The murderers have not been found.*

As you can see from the examples above, the subjects of these sentences are not specified, but are rather generic. This is when the **si passivante** enters the game.

📖 EXERCISES IV

1) Forma attiva E passiva? *Mark whether the following verbs have both an active AND a passive voice (AP), or just an active one (A).*

- Mangiare   (to eat)   _____
- Andare   (to go)   _____
- Vendere   (to sell)   _____
- Nutrire   (to feed)   _____
- Venire   (to come)   _____
- Alzarsi   (to get up) _____

2) Trasforma le seguenti frasi alla forma passiva. *Change the following sentences into the passive voice.*

Example: Il cane ha preso il giocattolo   <u>**Il giocattolo è stato preso dal cane**</u>
The dog took the toy.

- I fratelli hanno acceso la TV.   _____
  The brothers switched the TV on.

- La ragazza paga la borsa.   _____
  The girl pays for the bag.

- Il postino aveva consegnato il pacco.   _____
  The postman had delivered the package.

- Marco ha comprato una casa in città.   _____
  Marco bought a house in the city.

- Sara aveva trovato un gattino.   _____
  Sara had found a kitten.

UNIT 4

FUTURE TENSES

CHAPTER 1
FUTURE TENSE I

Now that you know how to talk about present and past events, it is time to start looking at the future! And, for once, this tense might be easier in Italian than in English.

In fact, in the English language, there are four main options when it comes to the future tense:

- *Simple present,* used to talk about scheduled events/actions in the future.
  For example, *the train leaves at 6.*

- *Present continuous,* used for plans and arrangements.
  For example, *I am playing the piano tomorrow.*

- *To be going to,* mainly used to talk about future intentions.
  For example, *this weekend, they are going to visit their grandparents.*

- *Will,* used for previsions, beliefs, willingness, promises and offers.
  For example, *he will help you with your homework.*

Basically, you pick the right form of the future according to the context of what you want to say. In Italian, if you want to say something about the future, you have fewer options. You either use the simple present or the future tense – **il futuro semplice**. This is why Italian students are upset when they discover the four options to build the future in English!

Before showing you the conjugation of the three groups of verbs in the future tense, a small clarification about the use of the simple present to talk about future actions/events in Italian. In general, when you can use the simple present in English, you can do it in Italian as well. The only exception is for sentences introduced by the word **quando**, *when,* which requires the future in Italian.

Examples:

- **Uscirai quando avrai finito di studiare.**   *You will go out once you finish studying.*
- **Prenderò la macchina quando avrò 18 anni.**   *I will get a car when I am 18.*

However, there are some instances where in English you would use the future tense, whereas in Italian you will need the simple present.

Examples:

- **Offro io!** *I will pay!*

- **Prendo un panino.** *I will buy a sandwich.*

To conjugate a verb in the future tense, once again, you will have to take the verb root and then attach the corresponding endings related to this tense. In the table below, you will find the conjugation of three verbs – one for each group – in the future tense.

SOGGETTO	TAGLIARE *to cut*	RIDERE *to laugh*	APRIRE *to open*
io	taglierò	riderò	aprirò
tu	taglierai	riderai	aprirai
lui/lei/Lei	taglierà	riderà	aprirà
noi	taglieremo	rideremo	apriremo
voi	taglierete	riderete	aprirete
loro	taglieranno	rideranno	apriranno

Have you noticed anything regarding the conjugation of the **-are** and **-ere** verbs in the future tense? Yes, their endings are the same! **-erò, -erai, -erà, -eremo, -erete, -eranno**. The endings of the -ire verbs are not that different. The only difference is that we have an *i* replacing the *e* of the other endings.

Examples:

- **Domani comprerò un nuovo tavolo.** *Tomorrow I will buy a new table.*

- **L'anno prossimo adotterà un cane.** *Next year he/she will adopt a dog.*

However, as you might expect, there are some irregular verbs as well. Let's start with the most irregular one, the verb *to be,* whose verb root changes completely in the future tense.

SOGGETTO	ESSERE *to be*
io	sarò
tu	sarai
lui/lei/Lei	sarà
noi	saremo
voi	sarete
loro	saranno

Of course, it is not the only irregular verb in the future tense. For example, there are some verbs that lose the vowel that joins the verb root and the ending of the future – as the *e* of **riderò**. We will conjugate the verb **andare**, *to go*, as an example of this irregular group of verbs.

SOGGETTO	ANDARE *to go*
io	andrò
tu	andrai
lui/lei/Lei	andrà
noi	andremo
voi	andrete
loro	andranno

If the verb *to go* was a regular one, the translation of *I go* would be **anderò**. Instead, the verb loses the *e* before the *r*, and it becomes **andrò**. The same applies to the following verbs as well:

avere   *to have*

cadere   *to fall*

dovere   *must/have to*

potere   *can/to be able to*

sapere   *to know*

vedere   *to see*

vivere   *to live*

Examples:

- **Domani potrò uscire con i miei amici.** *Tomorrow I will be able to go out with my friends.*

- **Farà bel tempo nel fine settimana.** *The weather will be nice on the weekend.*

- **Tra un anno vivranno in Spagna.** *They will live in Spain in a year's time.*

On the other hand, other verbs change their root when conjugated in the future tense. Please note that the same does not necessarily apply when conjugating the same verb in other tenses. In the table below, you will find some of the most common verbs belonging to this group of irregular ones.

SOGGETTO	VOLERE *to want*	VENIRE *to come*	TENERE *to keep*
io	vorrò	verrò	terrò
tu	vorrai	verrai	terrai
lui/lei/Lei	vorrà	verrà	terrà
noi	vorremo	verremo	terremo
voi	vorrete	verrete	terrete
loro	vorranno	verranno	terranno

You can see that the verbs above share a similar conjugation. The stems of these verbs would be **vol-, ven-**, and **ten-**, respectively. However, when you conjugate them in the future tense, you can see how the verb roots change to **vor-, ver-**, and **ter-**, respectively. Also, just like the other group of irregular verbs above, these verbs lose the vowel before the *r* as well.

Do not start feeling overwhelmed, we are almost done, we promise! There are still a couple of exceptions worth mentioning. The verbs ending in **-ciare** or **-giare**, when conjugated in the future tense, lose the *i* in the verb root. You will find two examples in the following table.

SOGGETTO	MANGIARE *to eat*	COMINCIARE *to start/to begin*
io	mangerò	comincerò
tu	mangerai	comincerai
lui/lei/Lei	mangerà	comincerà
noi	mangeremo	cominceremo
voi	mangerete	comincerete
loro	mangeranno	cominceranno

In fact, if **mangiare** were a regular verb in the future tense, the translation of *I eat* would be **mangierò**, with the *i* in the verb root – **mangi-.**

One last thing regarding the verbs ending with **-care** and **-gare**. These verbs, when conjugated in the future tense, require the addition of an *h* between the verb root and the regular ending of the future. Please find two examples below.

SOGGETTO	PAGARE *to pay*	CERCARE *to search/to look for*
io	pagherò	cercherò
tu	pagherai	cercherai
lui/lei/Lei	pagherà	cercherà
noi	pagheremo	cercheremo
voi	pagherete	cercherete
loro	pagheranno	cercheranno

Why do we need that additional *h*, though? It is a matter of pronunciation.

Let's take into account the infinitive of the verb to pay, **pagare**. You pronounce it *pah-gah-reh,* so the letter *g* has a hard sound. If we do not add that *h* when conjugating the verb in the future tense, *I pay* would become *pagerò,* and the pronunciation would change into *pah-jeh-roh*. You can see that the pronunciation of the *g* has changed. To keep the same sound of the infinitive form, we need to add that *h*. In fact, **pagherò** is pronounced *pah-gheh-roh.*

The same applies to the verb **cercare**, which is pronounced *cher-kah-reh.* If we do not add the *h*, *I search* would be *cercerò, cher-che-roh,* so the pronunciation of the verb root would change accordingly.

Before finishing this chapter, as usual, we will add a short list of useful words regarding the future. Perhaps you are already familiar with some of them.

domani	*tomorrow*
dopodomani	*the day after tomorrow (literally, "aftertomorrow")*
tra due giorni	*in two days*
tra tre anni	*in three years*
l'anno prossimo	*next year*
la settimana prossima	*next week*

As you might have noticed, **prossimo** follows the word it refers to, and needs to be adapted according to the gender and the number of the noun it refers to. For example, it's **l'anno prossimo** because **anno** is a masculine singular word. On the other hand, we must say **prossima** when referring to the week, as **settimana** is a feminine singular word.

Finally, did you know that the word **tra** has a double meaning? It can mean *in* – in terms of time – and *between/among* – in terms of space.

 **EXERCISES I**

1) Coniuga i seguenti verbi al futuro semplice. *Conjugate the verbs in the table below in the future tense. Beware, though! There might be some irregular ones.*

SOGGETTO	DIRE *to say*	APPOGGIARE *to place*	CONTARE *to count*
io			
tu			
lui/lei/Lei			
noi			
voi			
loro			

2) Traduci i seguenti verbi al futuro semplice. *Translate the following verbs in the future tense.*

- I will leave   _____ (partire)

- We will live   _____ (vivere)

- You will start   _____ (cominciare, tu)

- You will go   _____ (andare, voi)

- I will come   _____ (venire)

- She will do   _____ (fare)

- He will sing   _____ (cantare)

3) Ascolta l'audio. *Listen to the audio file and add the missing verbs in the future tense.*

Sono sicura che mia sorella _____ un ottimo medico. Diventarlo è sempre

stato uno dei suoi più grandi obiettivi, che _____ raggiungere l'anno prossimo.

_____ a lavorare in un ospedale in città, quindi _____ trasferirsi.

Io e i miei genitori _____ un po' tristi, ovviamente, ma _____

tutto il necessario per supportarla. Finalmente la _____ orgogliosa di se stessa!

Translation:

I am sure that my sister will become a great doctor. Becoming one has always been one of her biggest goals, which she will be able to achieve next year. She will start working in a hospital in the city, so she will have to move. Of course, my parents and I will be a little sad, but we will do everything we can to support her. Finally, we will see her proud of herself!

CHAPTER 2
FUTURE TENSE II

Known as *future perfect,* this tense is used when we want to talk about an action/event that will be completed at a certain point in the future, or before another action takes place – by the way, *will be completed* is an example of a verb conjugated in the future perfect tense. In short, when using this tense, there is a deadline for the action you are talking about.

Its construction is:

Subject + will have + past participle

Whenever you use the future perfect in English, you will have to use the corresponding future tense in Italian, the so-called **futuro anteriore**. This is how you form it:

(soggetto) + essere/avere al futuro + participio passato

As you can see, the structure of this tense is similar to the English one. The only difference is that you will have to choose between *to be* and *to have* as the auxiliary that needs to be conjugated in the future tense. Once again, you will pick **avere** if the main verb – the one conjugated in the past participle – is a transitive one, or **essere** if it is an intransitive verb.

If you do not remember the difference between these two verb categories, we invite you to review them in the chapter about the simple past (Chapter 1, Unit 3). *Oh!* And if you must use the auxiliary *to be,* do not forget to adapt the past participle according to the gender and the number of the subject.

Examples:

- **Tra un mese avrò finito il mio tirocinio.**
  I will have finished my internship in a month.

- **L'anno prossimo saranno sposati.**
  Next year they will be married.

In the following table, you will find two examples of verbs conjugated in the future perfect, one requiring the auxiliary *to have*, and the other one a reflexive verb that requires *to be.*

SOGGETTO	PERDERE *to lose*	STANCARSI *to get tired*
io	avrò perso	mi sarò stancato/a
tu	avrai perso	ti sarai stancato/a
lui/lei/Lei	avrà perso	si sarà stancato/a
noi	avremo perso	ci saremo stancati/e
voi	avrete perso	vi sarete stancati/e
loro	avranno perso	si saranno stancati/e

Please note that the verb **perdere**, to lose, has an irregular past participle – **perso**. As it requires the auxiliary *to have*, the past participle never changes.

The second example is the verb **stancarsi**, to get tired, which is a reflexive verb. We remind you that all reflexive and reciprocal verbs need the auxiliary *to be*. Also, never forget to add the reflexive pronoun. You can see the four options of the past participles, two for the singular and two for the plural.

Just one little exception regarding the use of this tense. Sometimes, in Italian, the future perfect might be used to make assumptions or a hypothesis about something that happened in the past. We know, it is weird, isn't it? In English, we would use the construction "must have…" in this kind of situation. This is all you have to know about the future perfect.

Examples:

- **Dove sono finiti? Si saranno fermati per strada.**

   Where are they? They must have made a stop on the way.

- **Luca ha chiamato. Si sarà dimenticato le chiavi.**

   Luca called. He must have forgotten the keys.

 **EXERCISES II**

1) Coniuga i seguenti verbi al futuro anteriore. *Conjugate the verbs in the table below in the future perfect. Beware, though! There might be some irregular ones.*

SOGGETTO	VENIRE *to come*	LEGGERE *to read*	LAMENTARSI *to complain*
io			
tu			
lui/lei/Lei			
noi			
voi			
loro			

2) Cosa farai/avrai fatto l'anno prossimo? *What will you do/will you have done next year? Try to write a short text using the simple future and the future perfect.*

_____

_____

_____

_____

_____

UNIT 5

CONDITIONAL & SUBJUNCTIVE TENSES

CHAPTER 1
PRESENT CONDITIONAL

The present conditional is a tense used to express a wish, a request or an offer, to give advice and recommendations, but it can be used for hypothesis and in indirect speech as well. Also, the present conditional is the tense we would use when we want to ask for something in a more polite way.

This is how you form this tense in English:

Subject + would/could/might/should + infinitive form of the verb

Examples:

- *We would travel all over the word, but we cannot.*

- *I could come to your place at 8.*

- *They might pick you up from the airport.*

Then, of course, the present conditional is used in conditional sentences, those with an *if clause* followed by the main one – as in *if you studied, you would pass the exam.* We will dedicate a chapter to conditional sentences at the end of the book, after introducing all the tenses required.

In Italian, the present conditional is called **condizionale presente**. Unfortunately, it does not work as in English, meaning that you cannot form it by simply adding *would, could* or *might* in front of the main verb of that clause. Otherwise, **sarebbe troppo bello per essere vero** – *it would be too good to be true.*

In order to form the present conditional of a verb, once again, you will have to attach the specific endings of this tense to the verb root. Let's look at the following tables, where you will see the conjugation of all three groups.

SOGGETTO	MERITARE *to deserve*	CHIUDERE *to close*	GUARIRE *to heal*
io	meriterei	chiuderei	guarirei
tu	meriteresti	chiuderesti	guariresti
lui/lei/Lei	meriterebbe	chiuderebbe	guarirebbe
noi	meriteremmo	chiuderemmo	guariremmo
voi	meritereste	chiudereste	guarireste
loro	meriterebbero	chiuderebbero	guarirebbero

We know, the conjugation of the present conditional in Italian seems very complicated at first. But trust us, it is not. As always, it is just a matter of practice.

The good news is that the endings for the **-are** and **-ere** verbs are the same! The endings for the **-ire** group are almost identical, though – you just have to replace the first *e* of the **-are/ere** endings with an *i*.

Examples:

- **Ti comporteresti meglio con i tuoi genitori?**

  Would you behave better with your parents?

- **Lavorerebbero solo la mattina.**

  They would work in the morning only.

- **Penseresti mai a noi durante il viaggio?**

  Would you ever think about us during your travels?

You know how it works. There is good news and bad news. And now it is time to reveal the bad news. As you might suspect, there are a few irregular verbs in the present conditional as well. We are going to group them according to the similarities they share, as we have done in the previous chapters.

Let's start with the usual two, **essere** and **avere** – *to be* and *to have.*

SOGGETTO	ESSERE *to be*	AVERE *to have*
io	sarei	avrei
tu	saresti	avresti
lui/lei/Lei	sarebbe	avrebbe
noi	saremmo	avremmo
voi	sareste	avreste
loro	sarebbero	avrebbero

If we take a closer look at the conjugation of to be, we can see that the verb root has completely changed. However, we are already familiar with this "new" verb root. Do you remember the conjugation of the verb **essere** in the future?

As with the verb to have, in this instance the verb no longer has the *e* belonging to the verb root. Once again, the same thing happens when we conjugate the verb in the future tense, as we have seen in the previous chapters.

Now, the second group is made of verbs which lose the last consonant of the verb root to add a double *r* instead. Let's look at two examples:

SOGGETTO	VOLERE *to want*	VENIRE *to come*
io	vorrei	verrei
tu	vorresti	verresti
lui/lei/Lei	vorrebbe	verrebbe
noi	vorremmo	verremmo
voi	vorreste	verreste
loro	vorrebbero	verrebbero

We have picked these verbs for two reasons. First, they are two of the main common irregular verbs in the conditional tense. Second, as the conjugation of these two verbs in the conditional tense is *veeery* similar – it is just a matter of a different vowel! – they are often confused with one another.

Also, the present conditional of the verb to want is very important, and you should learn it by heart. *Why?* Because Italians never say *I want,* as it is perceived as rude. They would always use the present conditional, which corresponds to the English *I would like.*

😆 **FUN FACT**

As children are inclined to say *I want* all the time, there is a common saying that Italian parents use whenever they hear the simple present of that verb instead of the present conditional. **"L'erba voglio cresce solo nel giardino del re",** which literally means *The "I want" grass only grows in the king's garden.* It is a metaphor to say that only the king is allowed to use the verb *to want* in the present tense, while everyone else should use it in the present conditional – *I would like,* **vorrei.**

Here are a few of these irregular verbs:

bere   *to drink*

rimanere   *to stay*

tenere   *to keep*

Examples:

- **Berrei caffè tutto il giorno!**   *I would drink coffee all day long!*

- **Terresti il mio gatto domani?**   *Would you look after my cat tomorrow?*

- **Non rimarrebbero mai da soli.**   *They would never stay alone.*

Here is the third group of irregular verbs in the present conditional. These verbs lose the first vowel of the conditional endings, the -e. Let's look at the two examples below.

SOGGETTO	ANDARE *to go*	POTERE *can/to be able to*
io	andrei	potrei
tu	andresti	potresti
lui/lei/Lei	andrebbe	potrebbe
noi	andremmo	potremmo
voi	andreste	potreste
loro	andrebbero	potrebbero

If these verbs were regular, *I would go* would be translated as **anderei** and *I would be able to* as **poterei**. Instead, the e belonging to the regular ending of the conditional tense has disappeared.

Here are other verbs following the same – irregular – rule:

dovere   *must/have to*

cadere   *to fall*

vedere   *to see*

vivere   *to live*

sapere   *to know*

Examples:

- **Dovrei studiare, ma non ho voglia.**   *I should study, but I do not want to.*

- **Vivresti mai all'estero?**   *Would you ever live abroad?*

- **Vedrebbero volentieri i loro cugini.**   *They would be glad to see their cousins.*

Forza e coraggio, siamo quasi alla fine!   *Be strong, we are almost at the end!*

As for the next group of irregular verbs, you already know what happens. We are talking about the verbs whose infinitive form ends with **-care** or **-gare**. Do you remember what we said while discussing the future tense? Those verbs need an additional *h* after the *c* or the *g* in order to preserve the same pronunciation of those letters.

SOGGETTO	PREGARE *to pray/beg*	CARICARE *to upload/charge*
io	pregherei	caricherei
tu	pregheresti	caricheresti
lui/lei/Lei	pregherebbe	caricherebbe
noi	pregheremmo	caricheremmo
voi	preghereste	carichereste
loro	pregherebbero	caricherebbero

As already explained, we need that *h* because the verb **pregare**, for example, is pronounced *preh-gah-reh*. Without the extra *h*, *I would pray* would become **pregerei**, which is pronounced *preh-jeh-reh-ee*. If we add the *h*, the verb is pronounced *preh-gheh-reh-ee*, meaning that the consonant *g* has kept its hard sound.

Other examples of verbs whose infinitive form ends with **-care** or **-gare**:

praticare   *to practice* (a very important verb for you all!)

giocare   *to play*

litigare   *to argue*

pagare   *to pay*

piegare   *to bend/fold*

Beware! When it comes to a musical instrument, you cannot use the verb **giocare**, but you must use the verb **suonare**, which is regular.

The next group of irregular verbs is made of very short verbs which keep their infinitive form, and then add the corresponding endings of the conditional tense without the leading vowel *-e*. Let's make it clearer with the examples below:

SOGGETTO	FARE *to do/make*	DARE *to give*
io	farei	darei
tu	faresti	daresti
lui/lei/Lei	farebbe	darebbe
noi	faremmo	daremmo
voi	fareste	dareste
loro	farebbero	darebbero

If you take a closer look, you can understand why we had to eliminate the typical *-e* introducing the endings. If we attach the regular endings of the conditional tense to the infinitive, we would end up with two letter *e*'s one right next to the other – **fare+ei** – which is a combination of letters that does not exist in the Italian language, so we need to delete one.

The same applies to the verb **stare,** *to stay,* and those irregular verbs with their weird endings in **-arre, -orre** and **-urre**, such as the following. We know that it is probably the first time that you are seeing these verbs, but please note that they are not that common. However, we felt that it is important for you to know that they exist and how to translate them!

distrarre	*to distract*	**tradurre**	*to translate*
attrarre	*to attract*	**produrre**	*to produce*
imporre	*to impose*	**condurre**	*to guide*
proporre	*to propose/offer/suggest (but you cannot use it to ask for someone's hand!)*		
supporre	*to suppose/assume*		

Examples:

- **Starei ancora, ma devo andare.** *I would stay longer, but I must go.*

- **Faremmo un grande sforzo.** *We would make a big effort.*

- **Supporrei che sia sbagliato.** *I would assume that it is wrong.*

One very last exception that you are already familiar with! The verbs whose infinitive form ends with **-ciare** or **-giare** lose the *i* of the verb root when conjugated in the present conditional, as we have already seen while discussing **il futuro semplice.**

SOGGETTO	BACIARE *to kiss*	DANNEGGIARE *to damage*
io	bacerei	danneggerei
tu	baceresti	danneggeresti
lui/lei/Lei	bacerebbe	danneggerebbe
noi	baceremmo	danneggeremmo
voi	bacereste	danneggereste
loro	bacerebbero	danneggerebbero

Examples:

- **Lascerebbe subito la città.** *He/She would leave the city immediately.*

- **Non lo bacerei mai!** *I would never kiss him!*

Now, take a deep breath and take your time to digest this "heavy" chapter before moving on. Once you feel ready, you will find a few exercises waiting for you on the next page.

REMEMBER!

Learning a new language requires <u>time and practice</u>. There is no need to rush.

 **EXERCISES I**

1) Coniuga i seguenti verbi al condizionale presente. *Conjugate the following verbs in the present conditional tense. Beware! There might be some irregular ones.*

SOGGETTO	VOLERE *to want*	CANTARE *to sing*	LASCIARE *to leave*
io			
tu			
lui/lei/Lei			
noi			
voi			
loro			

2) Cosa vorresti fare domani? *What would you like to do tomorrow? Write a short text using the present conditional tense.*

_____

_____

_____

_____

_____

_____

3) Ascolta l'audio. *Listen to the audio file and add the missing words.*

Tra un anno _____ di trasferirmi negli Stati Uniti. _____

iniziare una nuova _____ lì. _____ di trovare una casa a New

York, perché è una città dinamica con tante opportunità. _____ sicuramente

la mia famiglia e i miei amici, ma _____ che verranno a trovarmi presto!
Incrociamo le dita.

Translation:

In a year, I think I will move to the United States. I would like to start a new life there. I hope that I will find an apartment in New York because it is a dynamic city with a lot of opportunities. Obviously, I will miss my family and friends, but I believe they will come to visit soon! Fingers crossed.

CHAPTER 2
PAST CONDITIONAL

The past conditional is a tense we use in different situations. For examples, it is commonly used to describe what could have happened in a certain situation in the past, but did not occur – *I would have loved to go to South America!*

We can also use it to express regret or reproach – *You should have told me that he was not available.*

Also, the past conditional tense is required to form the so-called **periodo ipotetico dell'irrealtà** (unreal conditional clause), but we will focus on the conditional sentences after introducing all the tenses involved.

This is the structure of the past conditional in English:
Subject + would have/could have/should have/might have + past participle of the main verb

Moving on to the Italian language, the uses of the past conditional tense – **il condizionale passato** – are exactly the same, meaning that we use it in conditional clauses or to discuss something which was supposed to happen in the past – or that we thought could have happened.

Let's take a look at its construction:

(soggetto) + essere/avere al condizionale presente + participio passato del verbo principale

In order to form the past conditional, then, we need the combination of the auxiliary *to have* or *to be,* conjugated in the present conditional tense, with the past participle of the main verb. Once again, you will pick either *to be* or *to have* according to the main verb itself (is it a transitive or intransitive one?). However, if you use *to be*, do not forget to adapt the past participle according to the gender and the number of the subject the verb refers to.

The first thing we recommend, then, is to review the conjugation of the two auxiliaries in the present conditional (see previous chapter). Remember that some verbs might have an irregular past participle, so do not hesitate to take a look at the list at the end of this book in case of doubt.

In the following table you will find two examples of verbs conjugated in the past conditional, one requiring *to have* as the auxiliary, and the other one to be.

SOGGETTO	PARTECIPARE *to participate*	USCIRE *to go out*
io	avrei partecipato	sarei uscito/a
tu	avresti partecipato	saresti uscito/a
lui/lei/Lei	avrebbe partecipato	sarebbe uscito/a
noi	avremmo partecipato	saremmo usciti/e
voi	avreste partecipato	sareste usciti/e
loro	avrebbero partecipato	sarebbero usciti/e

Examples:

- **Avrei fatto le valigie nel pomeriggio.**   *I would have packed in the afternoon.*

- **Saresti passato comunque?**   *Would you have stopped by anyway?*

- **Avrebbero voluto viaggiare di più.**   *They would have liked to travel more.*

Now, what happens when a modal verb joins the team? For example, in the sentence: *they should have come earlier.* We all agree on the fact that in this clause there are three verbs: *should, have* and *come. To have* is the auxiliary verb in English, so you might be tempted to use the same one in Italian as well...

...But no! Keep in mind that the main verb of that clause is *to come. Should* – the verb **dovere** in Italian – is a modal verb, meaning that it "supports" the main verb of the clause. In a situation like the one above, with a main verb and a modal one, you will have to pick the auxiliary according to the first one. In this instance, then, you will have to choose the auxiliary according to the verb *to come* – **venire**, an intransitive verb of movement requiring the auxiliary to be.

And that's the final result:
Sarebbero dovuti/e venire prima.   *They should have come earlier.*

Let's take a closer look at the differences in terms of structure of the Italian translation. First of all, the subject pronoun is not needed. Then you can see the present conditional of the verb *to be,* conjugated according to the subject pronoun *they* – **sarebbero**. The past participle of the verb **dovere** follows the auxiliary, with the two options because we do not know whether *they* refers to a group of men and women, or a group of women only. The last element – just like in English – is the infinitive form of the main verb, **venire.**

After such a long chapter about the present conditional, we thought you might be relieved to know that this is all you have to know about the past conditional! Now it is just time for some practice.

 **EXERCISES II**

1) Coniuga i seguenti verbi al condizionale passato. *Conjugate the following verbs in the past conditional tense. Beware! Some verbs might have an irregular past participle.*

SOGGETTO	VESTIRSI *to get dressed*	AVERE *to have*	ESSERE *to be*
io			
tu			
lui/lei/Lei			
noi			
voi			
loro			

2) Essere o avere? *Pick the correct auxiliary verb for the following verbs and conjugate it in the past conditional tense. Beware! There might be some modal verbs and reflexive/reciprocal ones. You already know what to do, though ;)*

Example: ___**avrei**___ capito   *I would have understood*

- _____ partiti domani   *They would have left tomorrow*

- _____ mangiato una pizza   *I would have eaten a pizza*

- _____ venduto la casa   *We would have sold the house*

- _____ potuto fare un errore   *He could have made a mistake*

- _____ dovute rimanere   *You should have stayed*

- _____ lasciati prima   *We would have broken up sooner*

CHAPTER 3
PRESENT SUBJUNCTIVE

Now, as our old friend Dante Alighieri said, **"Or incominciano le dolenti note a farmisi sentire"**, a sentence that the poet said while approaching the damned souls in hell, and which could be translated as *Now I start feeling the sorrowful notes.*

Why quote Dante to introduce the present subjunctive? Well, it is not to discourage you, but we have to be honest. The subjunctive is probably the hardest Italian mood, and not only for English speakers. The same could be said even for Italians!

First of all, there is not a corresponding mood in English, which makes the situation a bit harder. The struggle, though, is not related to its construction. To build the present subjunctive, you will just have to learn the corresponding endings of the mood, as you have done with all the others.

When it comes to the present subjunctive, the hardest thing is probably understanding when to use it and then using it only when it is needed! But do not worry, we will take you by the hand during this journey. Also, keep in mind that, sometimes, even Italians get the present subjunctive wrong, so do not worry too much if you do not feel too confident!

Let's do a proper introduction. The present subjunctive is called **congiuntivo presente**. Its name comes from the old verb **congiungere**, which means to connect, to link.

Why is that so?

Because this tense is mainly used in a clause following the main one. More about it in a bit.

Second question: *What is this tense used for?*

The present subjunctive is used to make assumptions, when you want to say what you are thinking, feeling or hoping, and to express a wish or a belief. We also use it in conditional clauses, and this is why we decided to cover them at the end of the book, after learning this mood as well.

In order to explain this tense better, we will start with an example:

Penso che vogliano partire.　　　　　*I think they want to leave.*

You can notice the difference from the English sentence. In fact, in English, we would just use the simple present. Do not get us wrong: if you use the simple present in Italian too, everyone will still understand what you are trying to say. It is just… *ugly,* and not correct in terms of grammar. It is our duty, then, to explain the best way of expressing yourself in Italian.

First, let's split the two clauses:

Penso / che vogliano partire

The main sentence is made of one verb only, and it can stand by itself and make perfect sense – *I think.* Then we have the dependant clause with the verb **volere** conjugated in the present subjunctive. The important thing to notice is the word introducing the verb, **che.** All subjunctive tenses are introduced by that "che", which means *that*. That is a useful hint.

Since this tense is used to express someone's opinion, thoughts, feelings, ideas and hopes, it is useful to have a short list of verbs that can introduce a clause requiring the present subjunctive:

pensare	*to think*
credere	*to believe*
sentire	*to feel*
sperare	*to hope*
volere	*to want*
sembrare	*to seem*
dubitare	*to doubt*
temere	*to be afraid*
preferire	*to prefer*
dire	*to say*
immaginare	*to imagine*

Please note that this is not a comprehensive list of verbs requiring the present subjunctive in the following clause. These are just the most common ones. Also, remember that, in order to use the present subjunctive, the dependant clause must be introduced by *that,* **che.**

Besides the verbs, there are also some common constructions requiring the present subjunctive in following sentence or clause, such as:

è necessario che	*it is necessary that*
è possibile che	*it is possible that*
è probabile che	*it is likely that*
è improbabile che	*it is unlikely that*
essere contento che	*to be happy that*
mi dispiace che	*I am sorry that*
avere l'impressione che	*to have the feeling that*

Finally, these are some of the words introducing a clause requiring the subjunctive:

sebbene	*even though*
prima che	*before*
a meno che	*unless*
senza che	*without*
nonostante	*although*
affinché	*in order to*
a patto che	*on the condition that*
qualunque	*whatever*

Fiiinally, after this long – but necessary – introduction to the present subjunctive, it is now time to discover the conjugation of this tense! We will show you three examples of verbs conjugated in the present subjunctive, one for each verb group.

Once again, it all starts with the verb root. However, the only "unusual" thing you will notice is that, before the subject pronoun itself, we will add a **che**. This is how Italians learn the conjugation of this tense too, as the present subjunctive is often preceded by that relative pronoun (see above).

	SOGGETTO	DIGITARE _to type_	VEDERE _to see_	SERVIRE _to serve_
che	io	digiti	veda	serva
che	tu	digiti	veda	serva
che	lui/lei/Lei	digiti	veda	serva
che	noi	digitiamo	vediamo	serviamo
che	voi	digitiate	vediate	serviate
che	loro	digitino	vedano	servano

You have probably noticed that there is good news after all! The verbs do not change when conjugated according to the subject pronouns _I, you_ and _he/she!_ It is rather exceptional in Italian, but this is why you will have to specify the subject when using the verb conjugated according to these subject pronouns.

In fact, if you just say a sentence like **Spero che parta domani**, we do not know who you are talking about! It is literally translated as _I hope that leave tomorrow._ But who are you talking about? Is the subject pronoun _you?_ Or is it _he/she?_

The verb conjugated in the present subjunctive – as shown in the table above – is the same. This is why it would be better to specify it, for example by saying **Spero che TU parta domani**, _I hope that YOU will leave tomorrow._ Of course, sometimes there will be no need to specify it because the context makes everything clear already.

More good news: the endings are the same for the three verb groups!

Another thing to notice is that the verb, when conjugated according to the subject pronoun **noi,** is the same as the present tense.

Examples:

- **Penso che prendiamo l'auto.**   _I think that we will take the car._

- **Prendiamo la bicicletta.**   _We take the bike._

Now… you know this already. Take a deep breath before reading the irregular verbs in the present subjunctive. Do not worry, there are not too many, and they are not worse than the ones we have seen in the previous chapters!

Let's start with our usual two: **essere** and **avere**..

	SOGGETTO	ESSERE *to be*	AVERE *to have*
che	io	sia	abbia
che	tu	sia	abbia
che	lui/lei/Lei	sia	abbia
che	noi	siamo	abbiamo
che	voi	siate	abbiate
che	loro	siano	abbiano

Even though they are irregular verbs, the first three forms of the conjugated verbs follow the rules of the regular ones, and they are exactly the same. The same applies to the verb conjugated according to the subject pronoun **noi**, which is the same form of the present tense.

We will now show you the conjugation of the most used irregular verbs in the present subjunctive. Do not feel as if you have to learn them right away to be fluent in Italian. The learning process takes time. Take all the time you need to learn these verbs.

	SOGGETTO	ANDARE *to go*	STARE *to stay*	FARE *to do*
che	io	vada	stia	faccia
che	tu	vada	stia	faccia
che	lui/lei/Lei	vada	stia	faccia
che	noi	andiamo	stiamo	facciamo
che	voi	andiate	stiate	facciate
che	loro	vadano	stiano	facciano

	SOGGETTO	BERE *to drink*	VOLERE *to want*	DOVERE *must/have to*
che	io	beva	voglia	debba
che	tu	beva	voglia	debba
che	lui/lei/Lei	beva	voglia	debba
che	noi	beviamo	vogliamo	dobbiamo
che	voi	beviate	vogliate	dobbiate
che	loro	bevano	vogliano	debbano

	SOGGETTO	POTERE *can*	SCEGLIERE *to choose*	TENERE *to keep*
che	io	possa	scelga	tenga
che	tu	possa	scelga	tenga
che	lui/lei/Lei	possa	scelga	tenga
che	noi	possiamo	scegliamo	teniamo
che	voi	possiate	scegliate	teniate
che	loro	possano	scelgano	tengano

	SOGGETTO	USCIRE *to go out*	DIRE *to say*	VENIRE *to come*
che	io	esca	dica	venga
che	tu	esca	dica	venga
che	lui/lei/Lei	esca	dica	venga
che	noi	usciamo	diciamo	veniamo
che	voi	usciate	diciate	veniate
che	loro	escano	dicano	vengano

These are just some of the irregular verbs in the present subjunctive, but they are likely to be the ones you'll need the most.

Yes, you have to add an extra *h* to keep the hard sound of the infinitive form. We will just add a couple of examples to refresh your memory.

Then, of course, there is a final group of irregular verbs that you are already familiar with. Do you remember the verbs ending with -care or -gare? And more specifically, do you remember what happens when you conjugate those verbs?

	SOGGETTO	PAGARE *to pay*	CARICARE *to charge/upload*
che	io	paghi	carichi
che	tu	paghi	carichi
che	lui/lei/Lei	paghi	carichi
che	noi	paghiamo	carichiamo
che	voi	paghiate	carichiate
che	loro	paghino	carichino

We just need to add a few final points to remind you when you should use this (complicated) tense:

- When there is <u>uncertainty</u>. If you are talking about something sure, certain, you must use the simple present in the dependant clause, and not the present subjunctive.

Sembra che siano felici.   *It seems that they are happy.* (uncertainty)
Sono sicura che sono felici.   *I am sure they are happy.*   (certainty)

- When the subjects of the two clauses – main clause and dependant one – are different.

Spera che stiano bene.   *He/She hopes that they are well.*

- Please note that when the subjects of the two clauses are the same, you should use the construction **di**+*infinitive form* instead of **che**+*present subjunctive*.

Crede che non passi l'esame (NO) **Crede di non passare l'esame.** (YES)
She/He believes she/he will not pass the exam.

Great news: this endless chapter is now over!

 **EXERCISES III**

1) Congiuntivo sì o congiuntivo no? *Take a look at the following sentences with the present subjunctive. Write YES if the tense is correct, or NO if that clause requires another tense.*

· È necessario che lavorino sodo.   _____
  It is necessary that they work hard.

· Vedo che stiano giocando in giardino.   _____
  I see that they are playing in the garden.

· Mi sembra giusto che aspettino una risposta.   _____
  I feel it is fair that they wait for an answer.

· Sono certo che vada bene.   _____
  I am sure it's all right.

2) Coniuga i seguenti verbi al congiuntivo presente. *Conjugate the following verbs in the present subjunctive. Beware! Some verbs might have an irregular form.*

	SOGGETTO	VOLERE *to want*	SCRIVERE *to write*	FRIGGERE *to fry*
che	io			
che	tu			
che	lui/lei/Lei			
che	noi			
che	voi			
che	loro			

3) Finisci le frasi utilizzando il congiuntivo presente O l'infinito. *Complete the following sentences using the present subjunctive tense OR the infinitive form. Do not forget to add "che" or "di" accordingly.*

- Ogni mattina ho l'impressione _____

- Mi sembra che i miei amici _____

- Credo _____

- Immagino _____

- Penso _____

CHAPTER 4
PAST SUBJUNCTIVE

You read it right. The subjunctive tense is not over. *Do we really want to tell you that...* Yes, let's be honest. There are four kinds of subjunctives. But rest assured: the most difficult one is the present subjunctive, the tense we have already shown you in the previous chapter.

With this new chapter, you will discover the past subjunctive. And, luckily, there is not too much to say about it!

For starters, you will have to use it in the same situations we explained in the previous chapter, meaning that this tense is used to express something that is uncertain. The only difference with the present subjunctive is that, in this instance, we are talking about something that happened in the past.

Now, let's move on to its construction. Once again, you will find the past subjunctive in a dependant clause, which follows the main one. This is how you form this tense:

soggetto + avere/essere al congiuntivo presente + participio passato

As already mentioned, the subjunctive tense often requires an explicit subject, unlike all the other tenses you have already studied.

Then you will need the auxiliary verb, which can be either *to be* or *to have*. You will have to pick it according to the main verb of the clause (see the chapter about the simple past if you want to review how to choose it). However, the auxiliary will be conjugated in the present subjunctive. We remind you that you can review the irregular conjugation of **essere** and **avere** in the previous chapter.

Third element, the past participle. You already know how to form the past participle of irregular verbs, and, as with the irregular ones, the only thing you can do is learn them by heart.

The important thing to notice – which we have repeated multiple times – is that the past participle is invariable if we use *to have* as the auxiliary, while it needs to be adapted according to the gender and number of the subject if the verb requires the auxiliary *to be*.

To make it clearer, let's look at the conjugation of two verbs in the past subjunctive, one requiring **avere** as the auxiliary, and the other one **essere**.

	SOGGETTO	CAPIRE *to understand*	PASSARE *to pass by*
che	io	abbia capito	sia passato/a
che	tu	abbia capito	sia passato/a
che	lui/lei/Lei	abbia capito	sia passato/a
che	noi	abbiamo capito	siamo passati/e
che	voi	abbiate capito	siate passati/e
che	loro	abbiano capito	siano passati/e

Once you have learned the conjugation of the auxiliary verbs in the present subjunctive, it becomes pretty easy, doesn't it?

This is all you need to know about the past subjunctive in terms of grammar. To finish this chapter, we will show you a few examples of sentences requiring this tense in the dependant clause.

Examples:

- **Penso che Marta sia già uscita.**

   I think that Marta has already left.

You can see that, in this instance, we need the past subjunctive in the dependant clause, as the action of Marta leaving precedes the current action of me thinking. Please note that the past participle is in its feminine singular form, as the subject of the clause is Marta (female).

- **Suppongo che Luca abbia prenotato un tavolo.**

   I suppose that Luca has booked a table.

Once again, the action of booking a table precedes the action expressed in the main clause, so we need the past subjunctive.

- **Dubito che mio fratello sia già tornato a casa.**

   I doubt that my brother has already come home.

The subjunctive tense is required in the dependant clause because, once again, we are talking about something that is uncertain, as expressed by the main clause. Please note that the past participle is in its masculine singular form because of the masculine singular subject – *my brother*.

📑 EXERCISES IV

1) Coniuga i seguenti verbi al congiuntivo passato. *Conjugate the following verbs in the past subjunctive.*

- Partire, tu   _____

- Scrivere, noi   _____

- Preparare, io   _____

- Guardare, voi   _____

- Andare, lei   _____

- Chiamare, loro   _____

2) Congiuntivo presente o passato? *Complete the following sentences by adding the verb in the present or past subjunctive. Please note that some verbs may have an irregular past participle.*

- Penso che Maria   _____ ieri. (venire)

- Immagino che loro   _____ inglesi. (essere)

- È probabile che tu   _____ a casa. (restare)

- Credo che Francesco   _____ dall'influenza. (guarire)

- Dubito che i miei figli   _____ i compiti. (fare)

- Suppongo che l'insegnante   _____ una laurea. (avere)

3) Ascolta l'audio. *Listen to the audio file and add the missing words in the following text.*

Credo davvero che il mio migliore amico _____una persona splendida.

Non solo _____gentile e divertente, ma è sempre pronto

a _____in quattro per la gente che ha intorno. Penso che la

sua famiglia lo _____molto. Sono davvero grato di averlo nella

mia _____.

Translation:

I truly believe that my best friend is a wonderful person. Not only is he kind and funny, but he is always ready to go above and beyond for the people around him. I believe that his family has supported him a lot. I am very grateful to have him in my life.

CHAPTER 5
IMPERFECT SUBJUNCTIVE

Imperfect subjunctive, here we go!

You are already familiar with the imperfect tense, the lovely regular tense we explained in the second chapter of Unit 2. But what happens when the imperfect and the subjunctive become a couple?

Let's start by explaining when you should use this tense. Once again, it is actually easier than it might seem at first. We still have to use it while talking about some kinds of uncertain situations, just like the other two subjunctives you have already studied.

However, this time, the difference is in the main clause. You might have noticed that, with the present and the past subjunctive, the verb in the main clause is generally conjugated in the simple present. Well, if the verb of the main clause is conjugated in the imperfect tense, you will have to use the imperfect subjunctive in the dependant one.

Examples:

- **Penso che Giulia sia a scuola.**
  I think that Giulia is at school.

- **Pensavo che Giulia fosse a scuola.**
  I thought that Giulia was at school.

In the first example, the verb of the main clause is conjugated in the simple present, while the verb in the dependant clause is in the present subjunctive. In the second example, the same verb of the main clause is conjugated in the imperfect tense, and the verb *to be* of the dependant clause is now in the imperfect subjunctive.

Finally, we use the imperfect subjunctive in conditional clauses too. As anticipated, we will talk more about this in the final section of this book.

Now it is time to discover the conjugation of regular verbs in the imperfect subjunctive. Once again, it all starts with the verb root. Then, you will have to attach the specific endings of this tense, which are slightly different for each one of the three verb groups.

	SOGGETTO	ASCOLTARE _to listen_	VENDERE _to sell_	APRIRE _to open_
che	io	ascoltassi	vendessi	aprissi
che	tu	ascoltassi	vendessi	aprissi
che	lui/lei/Lei	ascoltasse	vendesse	aprisse
che	noi	ascoltassimo	vendessimo	aprissimo
che	voi	ascoltaste	vendeste	apriste
che	loro	ascoltassero	vendessero	aprissero

As you might have noticed, the endings are the same for the subject pronouns **io** and **tu** of each verb group. The other endings of the three groups are rather similar. The only difference is the first vowel of the ending, which changes according to the vowel of the verb group: **-a** for the **-are** verbs, **-e** for the **-ere** verbs, and **-i** for the **-ire** ones.

Examples:

- **Credevo che tu andassi all'università.**   _I believed that you were going to university._

- **Pensavo che cucinasse lei.**   _I thought that she was cooking._

Of course, there are some irregular verbs here as well. But beware! For once, the verb **avere** – _to have_ – is a regular one (**che io avessi, che tu avessi, che lui/lei avesse**, and so on). Let's look at the conjugation of the verb _to be_, which always tends to be a 'special' one.

	SOGGETTO	ESSERE _to be_
che	io	fossi
che	tu	fossi
che	lui/lei/Lei	fosse
che	noi	fossimo
che	voi	foste
che	loro	fossero

We have a few other verbs with irregular conjugation in the imperfect subjunctive. Actually, you already know some of them, as they are irregular when conjugated in other tenses too. Let's look at some examples.

	SOGGETTO	FARE *to do/make*	BERE *to drink*	DIRE *to say*
che	io	facessi	bevessi	dicessi
che	tu	facessi	bevessi	dicessi
che	lui/lei/Lei	facesse	bevesse	dicesse
che	noi	facessimo	bevessimo	dicessimo
che	voi	faceste	beveste	diceste
che	loro	facessero	bevessero	dicessero

Well, this is everything regarding the imperfect subjunctive.

Pronti per i nostri soliti esercizi? *Are you ready for our usual exercises?*

📑 EXERCISES V

1) Trasforma le frasi seguenti al passato. *Transform the following sentences into the past.*
You will have to change the tense of the verbs in the main clause and in the dependant one.

- Credo che tu sia felice.   _____
  I believe you are happy

- Penso che Laura parta alle 10.   _____
  I think Laura will leave at 10.

- Immagino che facciate i compiti.   _____
  I suppose that you are doing your homework.

- È probabile che lei venga al lavoro.   _____
  It is likely that she will come to work.

- Dubito che vivano ancora a Londra.   _____
  I doubt that they still live in London.

2) Completa le frasi seguenti. *Complete the following sentences using the present subjunctive or the imperfect subjunctive.*

- Penso che il mio gatto   _____
  I think that my cat...

- È possibile che l'anno prossimo   _____
  It is possible that next year...

- Credevo che l'essere umano   _____
  I thought that humankind...

- I miei amici vogliono che   _____
  My friends want (me) to...

CHAPTER 6
PAST PERFECT SUBJUNCTIVE

The past perfect subjunctive – **il congiuntivo trapassato** – is the last one, we promise!

And, along with the past subjunctive, it is one of the easiest tenses of this group.

Let's start with the basics. What do we use the past perfect subjunctive for?

Once again, we use it when we are talking about something uncertain that happened in the past, as we have seen with the imperfect subjunctive. However, in that instance, the action expressed in the main clause and the one in the dependant clause happen at the same time, in the past.

We will have to use the past perfect subjunctive when the action expressed in the dependant clause, requiring the subjunctive tense, happened earlier than the action of the main clause.

Examples:

- **Dubitavo che fosse in orario.**   *I doubted that she was on time.*

You can see that, in this example, everything happened in the past, but the two actions are simultaneous, so we need to use the imperfect subjunctive in the dependant clause.

- **Dubitavo che fosse partita in orario.**   *I doubted that she had left on time.*

Here the verb of the main clause is still conjugated in the imperfect tense, as in the previous example, but the action expressed in the dependant clause refers to something that happened before, hence it requires the past perfect subjunctive. This is the chronological order of the events: *she had left → I doubted that she had left on time.*

We are aware that this might seem quite complicated. You're probably wondering: *should I think about the chronological order of events for five minutes before I say anything?*

Well, when you start speaking in Italian, it is quite likely that you are going to do it. However, our advice is to <u>try</u> speaking right away. At the beginning, you will make some mistakes – it is obvious and, most importantly, perfectly normal – but then you will start understanding what to use and when, without stressing out too much!

That's all regarding the use of the past perfect subjunctive. Of course, this tense is also used in conditional clauses, which will be the main topic of the next – and final – chapter of this book.

As for its structure, this is what you need to form this tense:
soggetto + essere/avere al congiuntivo imperfetto + participio passato del verbo

In short, you will need the subject, then you will have to pick the right auxiliary – *to be* or *to have* – according to the main verb of the clause, and conjugate it in the imperfect subjunctive tense (see previous chapter). The last element you need is the past participle of the main verb of the dependant clause.

Let's look at two examples of verbs conjugated in the past perfect subjunctive, one requiring *to have* as the auxiliary, and the other one *to be.*

	SOGGETTO	SCEGLIERE *to choose/pick*	CADERE *to fall*
che	io	avessi scelto	fossi caduto/a
che	tu	avessi scelto	fossi caduto/a
che	lui/lei/Lei	avesse scelto	fosse caduto/a
che	noi	avessimo scelto	fossimo caduti/e
che	voi	aveste scelto	foste caduti/e
che	loro	avessero scelto	fossero caduti/e

Before showing you a few examples of sentences with the **congiuntivo trapassato**, do not forget to pick the right form of the past participle if the verb requires to be as the auxiliary.

Examples:

- **Ero contenta che il giudice mi avesse scelto.**
  I was happy that the judge had chosen me.

You can see how the action of the dependant clause – the competition judge making a choice – precedes the action expressed in the main clause – being happy because of that choice.

- **Pensavo che ti fossi dimenticato dell'anniversario.**
  I thought you had forgotten the anniversary.

Please note that the verb of the dependant clause – the one conjugated in the past perfect subjunctive – is a reflexive one.

 **EXERCISES VI**

1) Congiuntivo imperfetto o trapassato? *Add the missing verb in the following sentences, and decide whether it needs to be conjugated in the imperfect subjunctive tense or in the past perfect subjunctive. Please note that some verbs might have an irregular past participle.*

- Non sapevo che _____ al mare. (partire)
  I did not know they went to the seaside.

- Era probabile che _____ con noi. (uscire)
  It was likely that she go out with us.

- Pensavo che Marco _____ in Italia. (nascere)
  I thought Marco was born in Italy.

- Credevamo che _____ a casa. (essere)
  We thought you were home.

- Non eravamo sicuri che _____ un taxi. (chiamare)
  We were not sure if you called a cab.

2) A te la parola! *Write a few sentences using all the subjunctive tenses you have learned so far Good luck!*

- _____

- _____

- _____

- _____

- _____

- _____

- _____

CHAPTER 7
CONDITIONAL CLAUSES

Finally, now that you know *aaall* the Italian tenses, it is time to tackle the conditional clauses – **il periodo ipotetico.**

This construction is used to express a hypothesis - to talk about something that might happen, or might have happened in the past, or maybe that we wish had happened.

In English, in order to have this construction, you need two sentences:

If clause + main clause

The clause beginning with *if* expresses the hypothetical condition, while the main clause expresses the probable result.

In English, there are four main types of conditional clauses, with each type requiring a different combination of tenses. Let's review them together.

TYPE	USE	IF CLAUSE	MAIN CLAUSE	EXAMPLES
0	*general truth*	*simple present*	*simple present*	*If it rains, I get wet*
1	*possible condition + its result*	*simple present*	*future simple*	*If it rains, I will take an umbrella with me*
2	*hypothetical condition + its result*	*simple past*	*present conditional*	*If I had the money, I would go on holiday*
3	*unreal condition in the past + its probable result*	*past perfect*	*past conditional*	*If I had gone to university, I would have become a doctor*

Now, ready to discover how to make a hypothesis in Italian?

You have already done most of the work by studying all the tenses presented throughout the book. Now it is just a matter of putting them together!

First of all, as in English, in order to have a conditional clause, you need two sentences:

Protasi *(if clause)* + apodosi *(main clause)*

The very first thing you should learn, obviously, is the Italian translation of *if* – **se**.

Beware, though! Do not confuse it with the word **sé**, with the accent, which means *oneself*.

In English the *if clause* usually precedes the main one. In Italian, you can also find them inverted, with the main clause preceding the *if clause*, even though that is quite rare.

There are three types of conditional clauses requiring a different combination of verb tenses in Italian:

- **Periodo ipotetico della realtà**, is used to express a possible, realistic hypothesis.

  Example: Se corri, arriverai prima
  If you run, you will arrive sooner.

- **Periodo ipotetico della possibilità**, is used to express something that might happen.

  Example: Se avessi fame, mangerei qualcosa
  If I were hungry, I would eat something.

- **Periodo ipoterico dell'irrealtà**, is used to express an unreal hypothesis. For example, we are discussing something that could have happened in the past (but is no longer possible).

  Example: Se avessi studiato, avrei passato l'esame
  If I had studied, I would have passed the exam.

You might have noticed that there are quite a few similarities with the conditional clauses in English already! Now let's discover the tenses corresponding to the different types explained above.

TIPO	PROTASI	APODOSI	ESEMPI
PERIODO IPOTETICO DELLA REALTÀ	**presente o futuro**	**presente o futuro**	**Se esci con noi, ci farà piacere.** *If you go out with us, we will be happy.*
	presente	**imperativo**	**Se hai tempo, lava i piatti.** *If you have time, wash the dishes.*
PERIODO IPOTETICO DELLA POSSIBILITÀ	**congiuntivo imperfetto**	**condizionale presente**	**Se parlasse con te, non ci sarebbero fraintendimenti.** *If he/she talked to you, there would not be any misunderstandings.*
PERIODO IPOTETICO DELL'IRREALTÀ	**congiuntivo imperfetto**	**condizionale presente**	**Se avessi un milione, non lavorerei mai più.** *If I had a million dollars, I would never work again.*
	congiuntivo trapassato	**condizionale passato**	**Se avessi fatto più attenzione, non mi sarei fatto male.** *If I had been more careful, I would not have hurt myself.*

Conditional clauses are not that difficult in Italian, are they?

Generally speaking, we know immediately if we are talking about something certain, a real possibility, or something that will never happen.

And now you understand a bit better why we have decided to place our chapter regarding conditional clauses at the end of this *(amazing)* book – in order to make a hypothesis, you must know the subjunctive tenses!

😆 FUN FACT

The ugliest mistake you can make while talking in Italian is using the conditional tense in the *if clause*. In particular, there is one big mistake that makes one's hair stand on end... it is saying "**se avrei**", which literally means *"if I would have"*, instead of **"se avessi".** If you really love the Italian language, please never put those two little words together! The Italian **se**, when it comes to a possible or unreal hypothesis, NEEDS to be followed by the subjunctive tense, and never the conditional.

📑 EXERCISES VII

1) Quale periodo ipotetico? *Write if the following conditional clauses refer to a condition of reality (I), possibility (II), or unreality (III).*

- Se potessi, andrei subito in vacanza. _____

- Se fa freddo, metti un cappotto. _____

- Se lo avessi saputo, non saresti venuta. _____

- Se parlassi a voce più alta, ti sentirei. _____

- Se puoi, compra il pane, per favore. _____

- Se fossi più giovane, andrei a tutte le feste. _____

2) Completa le frasi seguenti. *Complete the following sentences by adding the right verb in the if clause and/or in the main one.*

- Se _____ un figlio, cambierei vita. (avere)
  If I had a child, I would change my life.

- Se fossero più studiosi, _____ già _____ gli studi. (finire)
  If they had studied more, they would have finished their studies already.

- Se Luca _____ meno timido, _____ più amici. (essere/avere)
  If Luca were less shy, he would have more friends.

- Se il treno _____ alle 3, _____ sbrigarmi. (partire/dovere)
  If the train leaves at 3, I have to hurry.

- Se vai in montagna, _____ tante foto! (scattare)
  If you go to the mountains, take a lot of pictures!

3) A te la parola! *Answer the following questions by using conditional clauses and as much vocabulary as you can!*

- Cosa sarebbe successo se non avessi studiato questo libro?
What would have happened if you had not studied this book?

_____

_____

- Cosa faresti se fossi miliardario?
What would you do if you were a billionaire?

_____

_____

- Cosa farai nel fine settimana se è bel tempo?
What will you do on the weekend if the weather is nice?

_____

_____

- Se potessi viaggiare ovunque nel mondo, dove andresti? Perché?
If you could travel anywhere in the world, where would you go? Why?

_____

_____

🎧 EXTRA
READING COMPREHENSION

Read the Italian translation of the tale *Little Red Riding Hood* – **Cappuccetto Rosso!** Underline all the verbs you find in the text. Then, on the next page, copy those verbs in the right column according to their tense. If you find the same verb multiple times, you can just add it in the corresponding column once.

Buona fortuna! *Good luck!*

"C'era una volta una dolce bimbetta; solo a vederla le volevano tutti bene, e specialmente la nonna che non sapeva più che cosa regalarle. Una volta le regalò un cappuccetto di velluto rosso, e poiché le donava tanto, e lei non voleva portare altro, la chiamavano sempre Cappuccetto Rosso.

Un giorno sua madre le disse: "Vieni, Cappuccetto Rosso, eccoti un pezzo di focaccia e una bottiglia di vino, portali alla nonna; è debole e malata. Sii gentile, salutala per me, e non uscire di strada, sennò cadi, rompi la bottiglia e la nonna resta a mani vuote."

"Sì, farò la brava," promise Cappuccetto Rosso alla mamma, e le diede la mano. Ma la nonna abitava fuori, nel bosco, a una mezz'ora dal villaggio. Quando Cappuccetto Rosso giunse nel bosco, incontrò il lupo, ma non sapeva che fosse una bestia tanto cattiva e non ebbe paura.

"Buongiorno, Cappuccetto Rosso," disse il lupo.

"Grazie, lupo."

"Dove vai così presto, Cappuccetto Rosso?"

"Dalla nonna."

"Che cos'hai sotto il grembiule?"

"Vino e focaccia per la nonna debole e vecchia; ieri abbiamo cotto il pane, così la rinforzerà!"
"Dove abita la tua nonna, Cappuccetto Rosso?"

"A un buon quarto d'ora da qui, nel bosco, sotto le tre grosse querce; là c'è la sua casa, è sotto i nòccioli, lo saprai già," disse Cappuccetto Rosso.

Il lupo pensò fra sé e sé: questa bimba tenerella è un buon boccone prelibato per te, devi far in modo di acchiapparla. Fece un pezzetto di strada con Cappuccetto Rosso, poi disse: "Guarda un po' quanti bei fiori ci sono nel bosco, Cappuccetto Rosso; perché, non ti guardi attorno? Credo che tu non senta neppure come cantano dolcemente gli uccellini! Te ne stai tutta seria come se andassi a scuola, ed è così bello stare nel bosco!"

Cappuccetto Rosso alzò gli occhi e quando vide i raggi del sole filtrare attraverso gli alberi, e tutto intorno pieno di bei fiori, pensò: "Se porto alla nonna un mazzo di fiori, le farà piacere; è così presto che sicuramente arriverò in tempo. E corse nel bosco in cerca di fiori. E ogni volta che ne coglieva uno, credeva che più in là ce ne fosse uno ancora più bello, correva lì e così si addentrava sempre più nel bosco. Il lupo, invece, andò dritto alla casa della nonna e bussò alla porta.

"Chi è?"

"Cappuccetto Rosso, ti porto vino e focaccia; aprimi."

"Puoi aprire la porta," gridò la nonna, "io sono troppo debole e non posso alzarmi."

Il lupo aprì la porta, entrò, e senza dire parola andò dritto al letto della nonna e la inghiottì. Poi indossò i suoi vestiti e la cuffia, si sdraiò nel letto, e tirò le tendine.

Cappuccetto Rosso poi si ricordò della nonna e si mise in cammino per andare da lei. Quando arrivò a casa sua, si meravigliò che la porta fosse spalancata. Allora si avvicinò al letto della camera e scostò le tende: la nonna era sdraiata con la cuffia abbassata sulla faccia, e aveva un aspetto strano.

"Oh, nonna, che orecchie grandi!"

"Per sentirti meglio."

"Oh, nonna, che occhi grossi!"

"Per vederti meglio."

"Oh, nonna, che mani grandi!"

"Per afferrarti meglio."

"Ma, nonna, che bocca spaventosa!"

"Per divorarti meglio!"

E come ebbe detto queste parole, il lupo balzò dal letto e ingoiò la povera Cappuccetto Rosso.

Poi, con la pancia bella piena, si rimise a letto, si addormentò e cominciò a russare sonoramente. Proprio allora passò lì davanti il cacciatore e pensò fra sé: "Come russa la vecchia! Meglio vedere se ha bisogno di qualcosa."

Entrò nella stanza e vide il lupo che cercava da tempo. Stava per puntare il fucile quando gli venne in mente che forse il lupo aveva ingoiato la nonna e che poteva ancora salvarla. Così non sparò, ma prese un paio di forbici e aprì la pancia del lupo addormentato.

Dopo due tagli vide brillare il cappuccetto rosso, e dopo altri due la bambina saltò fuori: "Che paura ho avuto! Era così buio nella pancia del lupo!" Poi venne fuori anche la nonna ancora viva. E Cappuccetto Rosso andò a prendere dei gran pietroni con cui riempirono il ventre del lupo; quando egli si svegliò, fece per correre via, ma le pietre erano così pesanti che subito cadde a terra e morì.

Erano contenti tutti e tre: il cacciatore prese la pelle del lupo, la nonna mangiò la focaccia e bevve il vino che le aveva portato Cappuccetto Rosso, e Cappuccetto Rosso si ripromise di non girare più da sola nel bosco, lontana dal sentiero, soprattutto se la mamma glielo aveva proibito.

IMPERATIVO	IMPERFETTO	PASSATO PROSSIMO	TRAPASSATO PROSSIMO	PASSATO REMOTO

IMPERATIVO	FUTURO	INFINITO	PARTICIPIO PASSATO	CONGIUNTIVO PRESENTE	CONGIUNTIVO IMPERFETTO

CONCLUSION

You made it!

You have just crossed the finish line, and we hope you enjoyed every single step you took.

Now that you have discovered the world of Italian verb tenses, **la palla è nel tuo campo** – *the ball is in your court!* We really hope that this journey made you even more motivated to learn this beautiful language and that you are now able to see how far you have come.

As we have repeated multiple times, learning a new language requires time, patience and much practice. Learning the verbs is one of the most important foundation bricks to build your Italian skills.

Before you go, here are a few tips we would like to give you:

- **Non sentirti deluso.**
  Do not feel disappointed if you think that you are not that fluent yet. The fluency will come. Just do your best to add more bricks to your building!

- **Usa tutte le risorse a tua disposizione.**
  Use every tool you can to include the Italian language in your everyday life. For example, watch films or TV series in Italian, but with English subtitles at first. As soon as you feel more confident, you can switch to watching Italian films/TV series with Italian subtitles. You will soon learn a lot of new vocabulary, and you will have the chance to work on your pronunciation too!

  Watch Italian videos, listen to Italian podcasts, read Italian books or newspaper articles... use all the resources the 21st century has given us!

- **Meglio poco, ma tutti i giorni.**
  Do not jump into long study sessions. Even though you might think that you are going to learn faster, that is not how it works. More likely, the only result you will get is feeling overwhelmed. Try to incorporate short study sessions in your daily routine. The key is being consistent! According to some experts, you need just 15-20 minutes of your time, every day, to learn a new language in a successful and long-lasting way. Only 15-20 minutes out of 24 hours!

- **Parla, parla, parla!**
  Do you have an Italian friend? If you do, you have our permission to 'use' him/her! Do not feel intimidated. In order to learn a new language, there is a very important thing that you must do: SPEAK!

- **Non avere paura di sbagliare.**
  Do not be afraid of making mistakes, and do not let those mistakes discourage you. Making mistakes is part of the learning process, and you will be able to learn thanks to those mistakes!

- **Scrivi quali sono i tuoi obiettivi.**
  Write your goals down. And we are talking about specific goals. Learning Italian, for example, is NOT a specific goal. On the other hand, learning 10 new words is a practical and specific goal. Or learning how to use the subjunctive. Doing all the exercises of a chapter of this book. Being able to watch a whole video in Italian, etc.

- **Festeggia tutti i tuoi successi, per quanto piccoli.**
  Celebrate every little accomplishment. Have you learned 10 new irregular verbs, or even 5? You should celebrate! Have you managed to understand an Italian text? Celebrate! Celebrating your accomplishments will keep your motivation up, and will make you realize that even if it might not seem like it, you are indeed making progress!

- **Non avere fretta di imparare.**
  Do not rush. Take your time processing all the new information. Practice. If you feel like you need more practice before moving on to a new topic, look for additional exercises and practice until you feel more confident. Moving on without having fully understood or processed what you have just studied is counterproductive.

Learning a new language is always a challenge. But that is what makes it such an incredible experience. One day, you will look back and you will give yourself a pat on the back. You have done such a great job already. C'mon, you have just read a whole book about Italian verb tenses!

And if you feel like you need some extra motivation – we all need it at a certain point, so you are not alone! – we have added a few motivational quotes on the next page **che stanno aspettando solo te** – *which are just waiting for you!*

Being your guides throughout this journey has been a real pleasure for us.

Grazie mille per averci scelto. A presto!
Thank you so much for choosing us. See you soon!

IF YOU NEED MOTIVATION...

On this page, you will find some motivational quotes that may help you when you are feeling like this is too much, or maybe when you think that you are not making any progress. Please know that it is perfectly normal to feel that way, but you also have to know that you ARE making progress! In those moments, you just need **una spintina,** *a little push,* so here you are!

- **La conoscenza non ha valore se non la metti in pratica.**
  Knowledge is of no use unless you put it into practice. (A. Checkov)

- **L'apprendimento è un tesoro che seguirà il suo proprietario ovunque.**
  Learning is a treasure that will follow its owner everywhere. (Chinese proverb)

- **Conoscere una seconda lingua significa possedere una seconda anima.**
  To know another language is to have a second soul. (Charlemagne)

- **Ancora imparo.**
  I am still learning. (Michelangelo)

- **Le lingue rassomigliano nel loro insieme a un prisma di cui ogni faccia mostra l'universo sotto un colore diversamente sfumato.**
  Languages look like a prism, and each one of its faces shows the universe under a differently nuanced color. (W. Von Humboldt)

- **Una lingua ti apre un corridoio per una vita. Due lingue ti aprono tutte le porte lungo il percorso.**
  One language sets you in a corridor for life. Two languages open every door along the way. (Frank Smith)

- **Una lingua diversa è una diversa visione della vita.**
  A different language is a different vision of life. (F. Fellini)

- **Non potrai mai capire una lingua finché non ne capisci almeno due.**
  You can never understand a language until you understand at least two. (G. Willans)

- **Sviluppa una passione per l'apprendimento. Se lo fai, non smetterai mai di progredire.**
  Develop a passion for learning. If you do, you will never cease to grow. (A.J. D'Angelo)

IRREGULAR PAST PARTICIPLE

INFINITIVE FORM	PAST PARTICIPLE
Aprire *(to open)*	Aperto *(opened)*
Accendere *(to switch on)*	Acceso *(switched on)*
Bere *(to drink)*	Bevuto *(drunk)*
Chiedere *(to ask)*	Chiesto *(asked)*
Chiudere *(to close)*	Chiuso *(closed)*
Correre *(to run)*	Corso *(run)*
Decidere *(to decide)*	Deciso *(decided)*
Dire *(to say/tell)*	Detto *(said/told)*
Dividere *(to divide)*	Diviso *(divided)*
Essere *(to be)*	Stato *(been)*
Fare *(to do/make)*	Fatto *(done/made)*
Leggere *(to read)*	Letto *(read)*
Mettere *(to put)*	Messo *(put)*
Nascere *(to be born)*	Nato *(born)*
Perdere *(to lose)*	Perso *(lost)*
Piangere *(to cry)*	Pianto *(cried)*

Prendere (to take)	Preso (taken)
Ridere (to laugh)	Riso (laughed)
Rimanere (to stay)	Rimasto (stayed)
Rispondere (to answer)	Risposto (answered)
Scegliere (to choose)	Scelto (chosen)
Scendere (to get off)	Sceso (got off)
Scoprire (to find out)	Scoperto (found out)
Scrivere (to write)	Scritto (written)
Spegnere (to switch off)	Spento (switched off)
Spendere (to spend – money)	Speso (spent)
Succedere (to happen)	Successo (happened)
Togliere (to take off)	Tolto (taken off)
Tradurre (to translate)	Tradotto (translated)
Vedere (to see)	Visto (seen)
Venire (to come)	Venuto (come)
Vivere (to live)	Vissuto (lived)
Vincere (to win)	Vinto (won)

Please note that this is not a comprehensive list of all the irregular Italian verbs. The verbs in the table above are just some of the most common ones. We don't want you to feel overwhelmed and, most importantly, we want to give you all the tools you need to start practicing and speaking right away!

ANSWER KEY

UNIT 1

1) scriveri, cucinara, studiaro, cuocera, spegnero

2) · dormire   **dorm-**
   · sistemare   **sistem-**
   · accendere   **accend-**
   · guardare   **guard-**
   · controllare   **controll-**
   · vendere   **vend-**
   · pulire   **pul-**
   · mentire   **ment-**
   · camminare   **cammin-**

3) • **Baciare**   *to kiss*
   • **Vivere**   *to live*
   • **Partire**   *to leave*
   • **Viaggiare**   *to travel*
   • **Imparare**   *to learn*
   • **Insegnare**   *to teach*

Exercises II

1) · I am playing basketball   **A**
   · She is young   **N**
   · Did you see him?   **A**
   · You have a big house   **N**
   · Don't smoke in here!   **A**

2) Oggi mi sento molto felice. **Ho** ripensato al mio ultimo compleanno e mi **sono** sentito molto fortunato. Sapete, ho molti amici che mi vogliono bene. Quando **ho** festeggiato i miei 30 anni, **ho** invitato tutti a casa mia per cenare insieme. Amo molto cucinare, e **ho** preparato la pizza per tutti! Ci **siamo** divertiti molto e **ho** ricevuto proprio i regali che volevo! Il vero regalo, però, era la presenza dei miei amici e della mia famiglia... E anche del mio cane! Sono la cosa più preziosa che ho. Adesso **sto** organizzando la prima vacanza che faremo tutti insieme. Non vedo l'ora!

Exercises III

1)
·	Devi cantare alla festa.	**dovere**
·	Vogliono andare all'università.	**volere**
·	Puoi ripetere, per favore?	**potere**
·	Vorrei un'aranciata fresca.	**volere**
·	Devo partire di corsa.	**dovere**
·	Posso cucinare io, se ti fa piacere.	**potere**

2) Io e la mia ragazza **vogliamo** organizzare le prossime vacanze. Pensiamo di andare in America del Sud, oppure **vorremmo** partire per l'Australia. Abbiamo lavorato tanto quest'anno per **poterci** permettere il viaggio. **Vorrei** prenotare un volo a inizio luglio, per poi tornare tre settimane dopo, sempre se **possiamo** prenderci così tanti giorni di ferie. **Dobbiamo** chiedere ai nostri capi se sia possibile o meno. Speriamo di sì! Sarebbe il viaggio dei nostri sogni, che **vogliamo** fare da quando ci siamo messi insieme.

Exercises IV

1)
·	Sposarsi	**REC**
·	Lavarsi	**REF**
·	Pettinarsi	**REF**
·	Incontrarsi	**REC**
·	Capirsi	**REC**
·	Mettersi	**REF**
·	Riposarsi	**REF**
·	Aiutarsi	**REC**

2)
Io	——	**mi**
Tu	——	**ti**
Lui/lei	——	**si**
Noi	——	**ci**
Voi	——	**vi**
Loro	——	**si**

3) Ogni mattina mia sorella **si sveglia** alle 7, ma non **si alza** mai prima delle 8. Poi **si lava** e va a fare colazione. Dopo **ci laviamo** i denti insieme in bagno e **ci prepariamo** per andare a scuola. I nostri genitori **si sono abituati** alle nostre facce assonnate! Prima che usciamo, ci abbracciano sempre.

1)
·	Prendere	**T**	*to take*
·	Andare	**I**	*to go*
·	Cambiare	**T**	*to change*
·	Guardare	**T**	*to watch*
·	Nuotare	**I**	*to swim*
·	Morire	**I**	*to die*
·	Vincere	**T**	*to win*
·	Atterrare	**I**	*to land*

2)
·	Andare	**Where?**	
·	Cambiare	**What?**	
·	Guardare	**What?**	**Who?**
·	Nuotare	**Where?**	**When?**
·	Morire	**Where?**	**When?**
·	Vincere	**What?**	
·	Atterrare	**Where?**	**When?**

1)
·	E poi sono uscita	**C**	*And then I went out*
·	La vita è bella	**M**	*Life is beautiful*
·	Perché non volevo	**S**	*Because I did not want to*
·	Quindi non sono partiti	**C**	*So they did not leave*
·	Hai visto i suoi amici	**M**	*You saw his friends*
·	Quando non lo sapevo	**S**	*When I did not know it*
·	Ma ci penserò poi	**C**	*But I will think about it later*
·	Il cane dorme sul divano	**M**	*The dog sleeps on the couch*

2) Quando **ero** una bambina / **pensavo** sempre al futuro. Il mio sogno **era** semplice: / **volevo diventare** una pilota di aerei / perché anche mio padre lo **era**. Nella mia camera **tenevo** tantissime miniature di aerei, / che **erano** davvero la mia più grande passione. **Avevo** anche altri sogni, però, / come **accogliere** tanti animali in casa mia / e **occuparmi** di loro. Se **avessi avuto** il tempo, / **avrei voluto** anche **imparare** una nuova lingua.

UNIT 2

1)

SOGGETTO	AVERE	ESSERE
io	ho	sono
tu	hai	sei
lui/lei/Lei	ha	è
noi	abbiamo	siamo
voi	avete	siete
loro	hanno	sono

2)
- I think **penso** (pensare)
- We do **facciamo** (fare)
- She eats **mangia** (mangiare)
- You drink **bevi** (bere, tu)
- He discovers **scopre** (scoprire)
- I go **vado** (andare)
- You choose **scegliete** (scegliere, voi)
- They sleep **dormono** (dormire)

3) Sono Francesca, **vivo** a Roma e **ho** 35 anni. Questa **è** la mia famiglia! **Ho** due genitori magnifici, Laura e Marco. I miei fratelli, Luca e Paolo, **lavorano** come camerieri in un ristorante famoso. Nel mio tempo libero, **faccio** sport due volte alla settimana e **vado** al cinema il venerdì sera. Il sabato e la domenica **esco** con i miei amici e a volte **incontro** gente nuova. **Adoro** conoscere persone straniere, perché **scopro** nuove culture e tradizioni, e **posso** migliorare il mio inglese!

Exercises II

1) La mattina **mi sveglio** alle 8, ma non **mi alzo** mai prima delle 8:30. Poi vado in bagno e **mi faccio** una doccia. In inverno **mi asciugo** sempre i capelli mentre mia sorella **si trucca**. **Mi vesto** per la scuola mentre i miei genitori **si preparano** la colazione in cucina. Dopo aver mangiato, **mi metto** il cappotto e sono pronto a partire!

2)

SOGGETTO	PETTINARSI *to comb your hair*	ALZARSI *to get up*
io	mi pettino	mi alzo
tu	ti pettini	ti alzi
lui/lei/Lei	si pettina	si alza
noi	ci pettiniamo	ci alziamo
voi	vi pettinate	vi alzate
loro	si pettinano	si alzano

3) *The exercise involves the ability to write a few sentences using all the information learned so far.*

Exercises III

1)
- They are watching   **stanno guardando**   (guardare)
- He is studying   **sta studiando**   (studiare)
- I am leaving   **sto partendo**   (partire)
- You are eating   **stai mangiando**   (mangiare, tu)
- You are paying   **state pagando**   (pagare, voi)
- We are dancing   **stiamo ballando**   (ballare)
- I am cooking   **sto cucinando**   (cucinare)

2)
- Next week I am going to the beach.   **F**
- I am studying Italian for my exam.   **PC**
- They are going home this weekend.   **F**
- She is getting dressed for tonight's party.   **PC**
- You are picking up the kids at 4 p.m.   **F**
- Sandra is planning her next holiday.   **PC**
- My cousins are visiting Paris.   **PC**

3) *The exercise involves the ability to write a few sentences using the present continuous in Italian.*

1)

SOGGETTO	BALLARE *to dance*	MUOVERSI *to hurry*	VINCERE *to win*
tu	balla!	muoviti!	vinci!
lui/lei/Lei	balli!	si muova!	vinca!
noi	balliamo!	muoviamoci!	vinciamo!
voi	ballate!	muovetevi!	vincete!
loro	ballino!	si muovano!	vincano!

2)
- He is in the classroom   **non parlare!**   (parlare, to speak)
- We are on the beach   **nuotiamo!**   (nuotare, to swim)
- You are running a marathon   **correte!**   (correre, to run)
- He is trying to learn Italian   **studia!**   (studiare, to study)
- You want to stay fit   **allenatevi!**   (allenarsi, to work out)
- He is lying   **non mentire!**   (mentire, to lie)

UNIT 3

Exercises I

1)

	AVERE	ESSERE
CONTROLLARE *to check*	X	
ABBRACCIARSI *to hug each other*		X
NASCERE *to be born*		X
STIRARE *to iron*	X	
PARTIRE *to leave*		X
ACCENDERE *to switch on*	X	

2)
- They discovered — **hanno scoperto** — (scoprire)
- She was — **è stata** — (essere)
- I drove — **ho guidato** — (guidare)
- Giulia and Martina went — **Giulia e Martina sono andate** — (andare)
- You saw — **hai visto** — (vedere, tu)
- You saw each other — **vi siete visti/e** — (vedersi, voi)
- He was born — **è nato** — (nascere)
- I watched — **ho guardato** — (guardare)

3) Ieri **è stata** una bella giornata. Io e mia sorella **siamo andate** in città per andare a trovare un nostro amico. **Abbiamo preso** la macchina perché ci vogliono trenta minuti circa per arrivare da lui. Quando **siamo arrivate**, Marco **ci ha servito** subito un buon caffè. **Abbiamo passato** tutto il pomeriggio insieme e **abbiamo visto** un film che **ci è piaciuto** molto.

1) · I was very shy at 18   **I**

· Yesterday they went to the cinema   **SP**

· She came, even if she had a meeting   **SP   I**

· We ate a delicious pizza   **SP**

· You traveled every weekend   **I**

· On Sundays, I slept until midday   **I**

· Did you meet Carlo this morning?   **SP**

2)

SOGGETTO	PARLARE *to talk*	CREDERE *to believe*	ESSERE *to be*	CUCIRE *to sew*
io	parlavo	credevo	ero	cucivo
tu	parlavi	credevi	eri	cucivi
lui/lei/Lei	parlava	credeva	era	cuciva
noi	parlavamo	credevamo	eravamo	cucivamo
voi	parlavate	credevate	eravate	cucivate
loro	parlavano	credevano	erano	cucivano

3) Quando **ero un** bambino, **sognavo** di diventare un medico perché **era** il lavoro di mio padre. **Ho** sempre **voluto** aiutare gli altri e fare qualcosa che facesse la differenza. **Ho studiato** per dieci anni all'università per realizzare il mio sogno. **È stato** difficile, ma non **volevo** mollare; **andavo** a letto tardissimo per studiare. **Mi sono laureato** l'anno scorso e adesso **ho iniziato** a lavorare in ospedale.

1)

SOGGETTO	VEDERE *to see*	CONCENTRARSI *to focus*	AGIRE *to act*
io	avevo visto	mi ero concentrato/a	avevo agito
tu	avevi visto	ti eri concentrato/a	avevi agito
lui/lei/Lei	aveva visto	si era concentrato/a	aveva agito
noi	avevamo visto	ci eravamo concentrati/e	avevamo agito
voi	avevate visto	vi eravate concentrati/e	avevate agito
loro	avevano visto	si erano concentrati/e	avevano agito

2) · Il campanello / ero / il postino / quando / uscita / ha suonato / appena

Ero appena uscita quando il postino ha suonato il campanello.

· quando / partiti / è / appena / sentito / erano / si / male

Erano appena partiti quando si è sentito male.

· invitato / cambiato / Luca e Marco / ma / idea / avevano / matrimonio / poi / hanno / al

Avevano invitato Luca e Marco al matrimonio, ma poi hanno cambiato idea.

Exercises IV

1) · Mangiare (to eat) **AP**
· Andare (to go) **A**
· Vendere (to sell) **AP**
· Nutrire (to feed) **AP**
· Venire (to come) **A**
· Alzarsi (to get up) **A**

2) · I fratelli hanno acceso la TV.   **La TV è stata accesa dai fratelli.**
· La ragazza paga la borsa.   **La borsa è pagata dalla ragazza.**
· Il postino aveva consegnato il pacco.   **Il pacco era stato consegnato dal postino.**
· Marco ha comprato una casa in città.   **Una casa in città è stata comprata da Marco.**
· Sara aveva trovato un gattino.   **Un gattino era stato trovato da Sara.**

UNIT 4

1)

SOGGETTO	DIRE *to say*	APPOGGIARE *to place*	CONTARE *to count*
io	dirò	appoggerò	conterò
tu	dirai	appoggerai	conterai
lui/lei/Lei	dirà	appoggerà	conterà
noi	diremo	appoggeremo	conteremo
voi	direte	appoggerete	conterete
loro	diranno	appoggeranno	conteranno

2)
- I will leave   **partirò**   (partire)
- We will live   **vivremo**   (vivere)
- You will start   **comincerai**   (cominciare, tu)
- You will go   **andrete**   (andare, voi)
- I will come   **verrò**   (venire)
- She will do   **farà**   (fare)
- He will sing   **canterà**   (cantare)

3) Sono sicura che mia sorella **sarà** un ottimo medico. Diventarlo è sempre stato uno dei suoi più grandi obiettivi, che **potrà** raggiungere l'anno prossimo. **Inizierà** a lavorare in un ospedale in città, quindi **dovrà** trasferirsi. Io e i miei genitori **saremo** un po' tristi, ovviamente, ma **faremo** tutto il necessario per supportarla. Finalmente la **vedremo** orgogliosa di se stessa!

1)

SOGGETTO	VENIRE *to come*	LEGGERE *to read*	LAMENTARSI *to complain*
io	sarò venuto/a	avrò letto	mi sarò lamentato/a
tu	sarai venuto/a	avrai letto	ti sarai lamentato/a
lui/lei/Lei	sarà venuto/a	avrà letto	si sarà lamentato/a
noi	saremo venuti/e	avremo letto	ci saremo lamentati/e
voi	sarete venuti/e	avrete letto	vi sarete lamentati/e
loro	saranno venuti/e	avranno letto	si saranno lamentati/e

2) *The exercise involves the ability to write a few sentences using all the information learned so far.*

UNIT 5

1)

SOGGETTO	VOLERE *to want*	CANTARE *to sing*	LASCIARE *to leave*
io	vorrei	canterei	lascerei
tu	vorresti	canteresti	lasceresti
lui/lei/Lei	vorrebbe	canterebbe	lascerebbe
noi	vorremmo	canteremmo	lasceremmo
voi	vorreste	cantereste	lascereste
loro	vorrebbero	canterebbero	lascerebbero

2) *The exercise involves the ability to write a few sentences using all the information learned so far.*

3) Tra un anno **penso** di trasferirmi negli Stati Uniti. **Vorrei** iniziare una nuova **vita** lì. **Spero** di trovare una casa a New York, perché è una città dinamica con tante opportunità. **Mi mancheranno** sicuramente la mia famiglia e i miei amici, ma **credo** che verranno a trovarmi presto! Incrociamo le dita.

Exercises II

1)

SOGGETTO	VESTIRSI *to get dressed*	AVERE *to have*	ESSERE *to be*
io	mi sarei vestito/a	avrei avuto	sarei stato/a
tu	ti saresti vestito/a	avresti avuto	saresti stato/a
lui/lei/Lei	si sarebbe vestito/a	avrebbe avuto	sarebbe stato/a
noi	ci saremmo vestiti/e	avremmo avuto	saremmo stati/e
voi	vi sareste vestiti/e	avreste avuto	sareste stati/e
loro	si sarebbero vestiti/e	avrebbero avuto	sarebbero stati/e

2) ·   **Sarebbero** partiti domani   *They would have left tomorrow*
·   **Avrei** mangiato una pizza   *I would have eaten a pizza*
·   **Avremmo** venduto la casa   *We would have sold the house*
·   **Avrebbe** potuto f are un errore   *He could have made a mistake*
·   **Sareste** dovute rimanere   *You should have stayed*
·   **Ci saremmo** lasciati prima   *We would have broken up sooner*

Exercises III

1) ·   È necessario che lavorino sodo.   **YES**
·   Vedo che stiano giocando in giardino.   **NO**
·   Mi sembra giusto aspettino una risposta.   **YES**
·   Sono certo che vada bene.   **NO**

2)

	SOGGETTO	VOLERE *to want*	SCRIVERE *to write*	FRIGGERE *to fry*
che	io	voglia	scriva	frigga
che	tu	voglia	scriva	frigga
che	lui/lei/Lei	voglia	scriva	frigga
che	noi	vogliamo	scriviamo	friggiamo
che	voi	vogliate	scriviate	friggiate
che	loro	vogliano	scrivano	friggano

3) *The exercise involves the ability to write a few sentences using all the information learned so far.*

Exercises IV

1) ·   Partire, tu   **che tu sia partito**
·   Scrivere, noi   **che noi abbiamo scritto**
·   Preparare, io   **che io abbia preparato**
·   Guardare, voi   **che voi abbiate guardato**
·   Andare, lei   **che lei sia andata**
·   Chiamare, loro   **che loro abbiano chiamato**

2) ·   Penso che Maria **sia venuta** ieri. (venire)

·   Immagino che loro **siano** inglesi. (essere)

·   È probabile che tu **resti** a casa. (restare)

·   Credo che Francesco **sia guarito** dall'influenza. (guarire)

·   Dubito che i miei figli **abbiano fatto** i compiti. (fare)

·   Suppongo che l'insegnante **abbia** una laurea. (avere)

3) Credo davvero che il mio migliore amico **sia** una persona splendida. Non solo **è** gentile e divertente, ma è sempre pronto a **farsi** in quattro per la gente che ha intorno. Penso che la sua famiglia lo **abbia supportato** molto. Sono davvero grato di averlo nella mia **vita**.

Exercises V

1) ·   Credo che tu sia felice.   **Credevo che tu fossi felice.**

·   Penso che Laura parta alle 10.   **Pensavo che Laura partisse alle 10.**

·   Immagino che facciate i compiti.   **Immaginavo che faceste i compiti.**

·   È probabile che lei venga al lavoro.   **Era probabile che venisse al lavoro.**

·   Dubito che vivano ancora a Londra.   **Dubitavo che vivessero ancora a Londra.**

2) *The exercise involves the ability to write a few sentences using all the information learned so far.*

Exercises VI

1) ·   Non sapevo che **fossero partiti** al mare. (partire)

·   Era probabile che **uscisse** con noi. (uscire)

·   Pensavo che Marco **fosse nato** in Italia. (nascere)

·   Credevamo che **tu fossi** a casa. (essere)

·   Non eravamo sicuri che **avessi chiamato** un taxi. (chiamare)

2) *The exercise involves the ability to write a few sentences using all the information learned so far.*

Exercises VII

1) ·   Se potessi, andrei subito in vacanza.   II

·   Se fa freddo, metti un cappotto.   I

·   Se lo avessi saputo, non sarei venuta.   III

·   Se parlassi a voce più alta, ti sentirei.   II

·   Se puoi, compra il pane, per favore.   I

·   Se fossi più giovane, andrei a tutte le feste.   III

2) Se **avessi** un figlio, cambierei vita. (avere)

· Se fossero più studiosi, **avrebbero** già **finito** gli studi. (finire)

· Se Luca **fosse** meno timido, **avrebbe** più amici. (essere/avere)

· Se il treno **parte** alle 3, **devo** sbrigarmi. (partire/dovere)

· Se vai in montagna, **scatta** tante foto! (scattare)

3) *The exercise involves the ability to write a few sentences using all the information learned so far.*

EXTRA

IMPERATIVO	IMPERFETTO	PASSATO PROSSIMO	TRAPASSATO PROSSIMO	PASSATO REMOTO
è	era	abbiamo cotto	era sdraiata	regalò
cadi	volevano	ho avuto	aveva ingoiato	disse
rompi	sapeva		aveva portato	promise
resta	donava		aveva proibito	diede
vai	voleva			giunse
hai	chiamavano			incontrò
abita	abitava			ebbe
è	sapeva			disse
devi	coglieva			pensò
guardi	credeva			fece
credo	correva			alzò
cantano	addentrava			vide
stai	aveva			corse
porto	cercava			andò
sono	stava			bussò
posso	poteva			aprì
russa	era			entrò
ha	erano			inghiottì
				indossò
				sdraiò
				tirò

				ricordò
				mise
				arrivò
				si meravigliò
				si avvicinò
				scostò
				ebbe
				balzò
				ingoiò
				si rimise
				si addormentò
				cominciò
				passò
				vide
				venne
				sparò
				prese
				saltò
				venne
				riempirono
				si svegliò
				fece
				cadde
				morì
				mangiò
				bevve
				ripromise

IMPERATIVO	FUTURO	INFINITO	PARTICIPIO PASSATO	CONGIUNTIVO PRESENTE	CONGIUNTIVO IMPERFETTO
vieni	farò	vedere	abbassata	senta	andassi
portali	rinforzerà	uscire	addormentato		fosse
sii	saprai	portare			
salutala	farà	fare			
guarda	arriverò	stare			
aprimi		filtrare			
		aprire			
		andare			
		sentire			
		afferrare			
		divorare			
		russare			
		puntare			
		salvare			
		correre			
		girare			

MORE BOOKS BY LINGO MASTERY

We are not done teaching you Italian until you're fluent!

Here are some other titles you might find useful in your journey of mastering Italian:

✓ Italian Short Stories for Beginners

✓ Intermediate Italian Short Stories

✓ 2000 Most Common Italian Words in Context

✓ Conversational Italian Dialogues

But we got many more!

Check out all of our titles at **www.LingoMastery.com/italian**

Made in United States
Troutdale, OR
09/21/2023

13064636R00097